PRAISE FOR *FOUNDI*

"With the verve of a storyteller and the precision of a historian, Paul Aron shows us how American politicians have been battling and backstabbing since the days when talking heads wore powdered wigs. Huzzah!"

—Gerard Helferich, author of *New York Times* bestseller *Theodore Roosevelt and the Assassin*

"Anyone who thinks the founders of the American republic were noble, selfless men ready to sacrifice private interests and personal opinions for the public good should read *Founding Feuds*. In lively prose and with keen understanding Paul Aron sets forth the personal animosities and grudges that drove politics in the new nation—often to distraction. Remarkably, for all the bitterness among these clashing personalities, the leaders of the fledgling United States were able to compromise with one another when necessary. Would that our preening politicians and self-centered ideologues could do the same!"

—Robert Gross, author of *The Minutemen and Their World*

"By focusing on the internal conflicts that nearly tore the fledging United States to shreds, Paul Aron provides an excellent entrée into the world of the founding fathers. He strips these stories to their essentials without dumbing them down. And by summing up each struggle as a contest between two outsized eighteenth-century characters, he draws us readers right into the fray. As the sparks fly, they light up the scene."

)f *Abigail Adams*

"Through his lively and often surprising descriptions of the founders' brawls, disagreements, public denunciations, court battles, and lethal duels, Paul Aron makes the important argument that many of their feuds actually strengthened the young republic and that our robust, open democracy is in fact built on an agreement to disagree."

—Susan Dunn, author of *Dominion of Memories*

"Paul Aron's lively *Founding Feuds* should reassure readers that the political stridency of the present is an essential part of our tradition."

—Richard Buel, author of *America on the Brink*

"Those who think nastiness is a recent addition to our politics should read this book. *Founding Feuds* reminds us that mud-slinging goes back to the beginnings of the American republic."

—John Mack Faragher, author of *Eternity Street*

"*Founding Feuds* is a sprightly and insightful account of multiple rivalries and rancorous disputes involving many of America's founding fathers and mothers. Paul Aron's lucid and engaging style, and his informed understanding of these bitter conflicts, makes for good reading. I recommend *Founding Feuds* to all who wish to learn more about the era of the American Revolution and many of its most important players."

—John Ferling, author of *Whirlwind*

FOUNDING FEUDS

✦ ✦ ✦

The Rivalries, Clashes,
and Conflicts That Forged a Nation

PAUL ARON

Colonial Williamsburg

Published by Sourcebooks, Inc.
P.O. Box 4410, Naperville, Illinois 60567-4410
(630) 961-3900
Fax: (630) 961-2168
www.sourcebooks.com

Library of Congress Cataloging-in-Publication Data

Names: Aron, Paul, author.
Title: Founding feuds : the rivalries, clashes, and conflicts that forged a
   nation / Paul Aron.
Description: Naperville, Illinois : Sourcebooks, 2016. | Includes
   bibliographical references and index.
Identifiers: LCCN 2015050177 (pbk. : alk. paper)
Subjects: LCSH: United States--Politics and government--1783-1809. | United
   States--Politics and government--1775-1783. | National characteristics,
   American--History. | Founding Fathers of the United States.
Classification: LCC E310 .A76 2016 | DDC 973.3092/2--dc23 LC record available at http://
lccn.loc.gov/2015050177

Printed and bound in the United States of America.
VP 10 9 8 7 6 5 4 3 2 1

33614057653551

CONTENTS

PREFACE

"THIRTEEN CLOCKS WERE MADE TO STRIKE TOGETHER," John Adams wrote in 1818, recalling how the thirteen colonies united to seize their independence.

Adams knew this had been a tentative and tenuous unity. On July 1, the day before the colonists would vote for independence, John Dickinson of Pennsylvania had argued for delay, mustering the same arguments moderates had been making in the Continental Congress for months: that it might still be possible to reconcile with England, that Americans were not yet united behind independence, that America needed allies and troops before it could take on the world's most powerful empire. To take on England prematurely, Dickinson said, would be "to brave the storm in a skiff made of paper."

The day of the vote, Delaware supported independence only because of the last-minute arrival of Caesar Rodney, who had ridden through the night to break a tie among that colony's delegates. Pennsylvania supported independence only because

Dickinson and fellow moderate James Wilson chose not to participate. And New York abstained, meaning one of Adams's thirteen clocks struck not at all.

Still, Adams was right to recall that, in July 1776, a great many Americans rallied round the cause. Dickinson, despite refusing to sign the Declaration of Independence, served as commander of a Philadelphia battalion and chaired the city's committee responsible for raising troops and building fortifications. That even twelve clocks struck together was, as Adams wrote, "a perfection of mechanism, which no artist had ever before effected."

Or, perhaps, ever again effected—for the unity did not last and has only rarely returned. "The progress of evolution from President Washington to President Grant," wrote Henry Adams, famed historian and John's great-grandson, "was alone evidence enough to upset Darwin."

Most Americans would agree that the history of the nation's leadership has hardly been an example of evolutionary progress. Mired in gridlock and repulsed by partisan bickering, we long for an era when our politicians were statesmen and philosophers.

These longings can blind us to the reality that our founders were as apt to disagree with each other as any twenty-first-century Democrats and Republicans, and their disagreements were at least as heated. Their feuds were driven by ideological differences, to be sure, but also by personal ambitions. And they were by no means above attacking their opponents, spreading stories of scandals both true and untrue, playing on voters' emotions, and manipulating the electoral system. At stake, they believed, was the nature—indeed the survival—of the American republic.

Take, for example, Alexander Hamilton and Thomas Jefferson. Hamilton thought Jefferson would import the terror of the French Revolution to America. Jefferson thought Hamilton would turn America into a monarchy. When Hamilton was secretary of the treasury and Jefferson secretary of state, George Washington attempted to mediate, with little success.

During the Revolution, Hamilton had served in the Continental Army. Jefferson spent much of the war at home. When British forces approached Monticello, Jefferson galloped away. Or, as Hamilton put it, "The governor of the ancient dominion dwindled into the poor, timid philosopher, and instead of rallying his brave countrymen, he fled for safety from a few light horsemen."

For his part, Jefferson called Hamilton "a man whose history, from the moment at which history can stoop to notice him, is a tissue of machinations against the liberty of the country which has not only received and given him bread, but heaped its honors on his head." When Hamilton caught yellow fever, Jefferson accused him of hypochondria.

The stakes were just as high when Jefferson feuded with John Adams. Jefferson referred to his victory over Adams in their second presidential contest as "the revolution of 1800, for that was as real a revolution in the principles of our government as that of 1776 was in its form." Adams was never at a loss for words, but his thoughts about the election results were best expressed by his actions. On the day of Jefferson's inauguration, March 4, 1801, Adams took the four-a.m. stage home to Massachusetts. He never returned to Washington.

Given the intensity of Jefferson's feuds with Hamilton and with Adams, you might assume—on the hypothesis that "the enemy of my enemy is my friend"—that Hamilton and Adams were at least allies. Not so: Hamilton and Adams despised each other. Hamilton wrote publicly of "the disgusting egotism, the distempered jealousy, and the ungovernable indiscretion of Mr. Adams's temper." Adams responded by calling Hamilton "an insolent coxcomb" and, revealing his intolerance for those born outside marriage and outside America, "a bastard brat of a Scotch peddler."

The founders' feuds extended well beyond Adams and Hamilton and Jefferson, and the wars of words occasionally turned violent, even in the halls of Congress. In 1798, Congressman Roger Griswold of Connecticut got in about twenty blows with his cane before Congressman Matthew Lyon of Vermont could fend him off with some fireplace tongs. Most famously, in 1804, Vice President Aaron Burr shot and killed Alexander Hamilton.

"Men who have been intimate all their lives cross the streets to avoid meeting, and turn their heads another way, lest they should be obliged to touch their hat," wrote Jefferson in 1797. The founders spent so much time insulting each other that in 1807 Washington Irving's satirical magazine, *Salmagundi*, described the government as "a pure unadulterated logocracy."

I hope you will find the stories of our founders' feuds revealing about their ideas and their passions. Perhaps, too, you will also find here some signs of hope for our own times. After all, despite their constant feuding—in many ways *because* of these feuds—the founders managed to build a nation and inspire generations.

"The American experiment is, at its soul, an enduring debate," wrote educators H. Michael Hartoonian, Richard D. Van Scotter, and William White in *The Idea of America*. That our own debates are as impassioned as those of the founders means that this experiment, far from having failed, continues.

SILAS DEANE

✦ ━━━━━━━━━━ *and* ━━━━━━━━━━ ✦

ARTHUR LEE

His countenance is disgusting, his air is not pleasing, his manners are not engaging, his temper is harsh, sour, and fiery.

JOHN ADAMS ON ARTHUR LEE

What Mr. Deane's political principles were if he had any I never could learn. His views always appeared to me commercial and interested.

SAMUEL ADAMS ON SILAS DEANE

FACED WITH THE OVERWHELMING SUPERIORITY OF THE BRITISH military, the Continental Congress sent a secret agent to France in early 1776 to negotiate for diplomatic support, weapons, and other materials. This was Silas Deane, a merchant and former delegate to Congress who, along with Benedict Arnold, had been instrumental in the capture of Fort Ticonderoga from the British. Deane's cover story was that he was representing the trading firm of Morris and Willing.

Deane was an unlikely agent: he had lived most of his life in

Connecticut and spoke not a word of French. Benjamin Franklin thought Deane's best qualification for the job was that he was so clearly unqualified to be a secret agent that no one would suspect him of anything other than working for Morris and Willing.

In Paris, Deane found a partner with the court savvy he lacked. Pierre-Augustin Caron de Beaumarchais was at various times a watchmaker, a spy, a diplomat, and a playwright; he created the character of Figaro, who inspired operas by both Mozart and Rossini. Beaumarchais was also an arms dealer. Deane and Beaumarchais worked out a deal to send cannons, muskets, ammunition, and clothing to the Continental Army. Since American money was virtually worthless, Congress would pay for all this with tobacco.

Amidst the complex negotiations, Congress appointed Benjamin Franklin and Arthur Lee to join Deane as America's commissioners to France. The mission was no longer secret; Franklin was too big a celebrity to go unnoticed. As for Lee, he was the youngest son in a wealthy and distinguished Virginia family. His brother, Richard Henry Lee, had introduced the motion for independence in Congress. Arthur Lee's intelligence was undeniable—he was both a doctor and a lawyer—but it was, unfortunately, matched by his arrogance and tactlessness. John Adams, who generally allied himself with the Lees in Congress, said of Arthur Lee that "his judgment of men and things is often wrong."

Franklin set about charming the French court and nation. Lee quickly offended both French diplomats and his fellow American commissioners, especially Deane. When the feud between Deane and Lee spilled over into the halls of Congress, it split its members publicly as no issue had since independence.

⬥◼◼◼⬥

EVEN BEFORE LEE ARRIVED IN PARIS, HE WAS DISTRESSED BY DEANE'S dealings with Beaumarchais. Lee had met Beaumarchais in London in 1775 and, without authorization from Congress, had taken it upon himself to negotiate an arms-for-tobacco deal. Nothing had come of those negotiations, but Lee worried that Deane might get the credit for his earlier efforts. Deane and Franklin further antagonized Lee by largely excluding him from their negotiations with the French.

Deane's and Franklin's negotiations paid off in 1777, when Beaumarchais's ships sailed to America loaded with arms and other material for the army. The material made its way to Saratoga, as did American volunteers, encouraged by word that they had what they needed to fight the British. The American victory at Saratoga that fall was a turning point in the war. After Saratoga, British military operations were largely limited to the South.

The victory didn't stop Lee from complaining to his brothers and others in Congress. He accused both Deane and Franklin of profiting personally from the French deals. He claimed there was no reason to pay Beaumarchais, since the arms were a gift from the French government. And he accused Edward Bancroft, the secretary to the American commissioners, of being a British spy. This last accusation turned out to be true, as British archives revealed when they were made public a century later.

Deane was increasingly exasperated. Lee "must be shaved and bled, or he will actually be made for life," Deane wrote in January 1778. Franklin stopped answering Lee's letters, explaining that he did so because of "my pity of your sick mind, which is forever tormenting itself, with jealousies, suspicions and fancies that others mean you ill, wrong you, or fail in respect for you."

Lee's complaints ultimately forced Congress to act. In early 1778, Congress recalled Deane from France, replacing him with John Adams, and opened an investigation into Deane's conduct.

Lee's supporters in Congress charged that Deane had granted nearly sixty commissions to French gentlemen, making them officers in the Continental Army even though many were unqualified and the army could not afford to pay them. This was true, though Deane thought his actions necessary to gain the favor of the French court. Besides, not all his commissions turned out to be problems; among the Frenchmen who joined the Continental Army was the Marquis de Lafayette, who became one of Washington's most trusted officers.

The more serious accusation was that Deane had used his mission for personal profit. Richard Henry Lee called as a witness William Carmichael, a merchant who had worked as secretary to Deane and Franklin. Lee announced to Congress that Carmichael would show that "Deane had misapplied the public money." Carmichael's actual testimony was inconclusive, since he admitted he did not recall many details of Deane's transactions. Arthur Lee's supporters also introduced Arthur's own letters as evidence, though these were too obviously biased to be of much use as evidence.

Beaumarchais rose to Deane's defense. In a letter to Congress, he wrote that he had arranged for the arms shipments after Deane had promised him Congress would pay for them. Beaumarchais added, "I certify that if my zeal, my money advances, and shipments of munitions and merchandise have been agreeable to the noble Congress, their gratitude is due to the indefatigable exertions of Mr. Deane."

Franklin, too, wrote on Deane's behalf, calling him "a faithful, active, and able minister, who to my knowledge has done in various ways great and important services to his country."

Also testifying on Deane's behalf was Conrad Gerard, the new French ambassador. He reiterated that the French government wanted nothing more to do with Arthur Lee.

Appearing before Congress, Deane stressed that he was eager to show that he had not "applied one shilling of the public moneys to my own use." He added, "It is well known that my private fortune in America, which at the time I left my country was moderate, has not been augmented, but the contrary, by my absence." He had brought virtually nothing back from France "excepting my clothes."

Deane's defense was hampered by having left his account books in France. Even if he had brought them, they would have been confusing. In order to conceal the secret arms deals and preserve his initial cover story that he was merely an agent for Morris and Willing,

Deane had mixed his public and private transactions. It also didn't help his case that, while waiting to testify before Congress, Deane lodged with Benedict Arnold. Arnold had not yet turned traitor, but his opulent lifestyle and his flirtation with a loyalist's daughter made him an object of suspicion.

Both sides took their case to the public. In an essay in the *Pennsylvania Packet*, Deane blamed Lee for almost derailing the mission by offending the French and charged him with passing on intelligence to the British. He accused Congress of refusing to hear his side of the story, since "their ears have been shut against me."

The Lees and their supporters recruited Thomas Paine to write a response in the same newspaper. Paine was appalled by Deane's "barbarous, unmanly, and unsupported attack" on Lee. Paine repeated Lee's claims that the French military supplies had been a gift, that there was no need to repay Beaumarchais, and that Deane had embezzled public funds. Lest there be any doubt of his credentials, Paine signed off as "Common Sense," the title of the pamphlet he'd written that many credited with inspiring Americans to support the Revolution.

The feud between Deane and Lee polarized Congress as never before. John Adams feared the affair would end with either "the ruin of Mr. Deane, or the ruin of his country." George Washington moaned that "party disputes and personal quarrels are the great business of the day whilst the momentous concerns of an empire—a great and accumulated debt—ruined finances—depreciated money—and want of credit…are but secondary considerations and postponed…as if our affairs wore the most promising aspect."

This was clearly more than a matter of difficult personalities, however disagreeable Lee was. The Lees and their supporters were appalled by the way Deane mixed personal and government business. "What Mr. Deane's political principles were if he had any I never could learn," wrote Samuel Adams. "His views always appeared to me commercial and interested." Asked Paine: "To what a degree of corruption must we sink if our delegates and ambassadors are to be admitted to carry on a private partnership in trade?"

For Robert Morris, who was a signer of the Declaration of Independence as well as a partner in the firm that had provided Deane's cover story in France, there was no conflict between the pursuit of private wealth and the nation's interest. "I do not conceive that the state I live in has any right or inclination to enquire into what mercantile connection I have had or now have with Mr. Deane or with any other person," he wrote. "As I did not, by becoming a delegate for the state of Pennsylvania, relinquish my right of forming mercantile connections, I was unquestionably at liberty to form such with Mr. Deane."

The divide was also regional. Like most of those who supported John Adams and Richard Henry Lee in their fight for a declaration of independence, Arthur Lee's supporters came mostly from the states of New England and the South, whose wealth came primarily from agriculture. Deane's supporters were mostly from New York, Pennsylvania, and Maryland, where commercial and financial interests were more dominant. The economic problems brought on by the Revolution exacerbated these tensions.

THE LEES HAD RESENTED FRANKLIN SINCE THE EARLY 1770S, when he had represented a company that was competing with the Lees for a grant of land in the Ohio Valley. In September 1778, Richard Henry Lee wrote Arthur Lee that Franklin was "immoral" and that "the doctor is old and must soon be called to account for his misdeeds." But in publicly attacking Franklin—already an American icon—the Lees went too far. They alienated potential congressional allies and ended up strengthening support for Deane.

And, overall, Deane's defense in Congress was convincing. In January 1779, Congress unanimously agreed that Lee's claim that the French supplies were a present was untrue. Indeed, the debate in Congress turned from Deane's conduct to Lee's, and a vote to recall Lee from France failed by a single vote.

Lee's reputation never recovered. He was elected to Congress in 1781 but then further alienated many of his family's previous allies, including Thomas Jefferson and James Madison. He made clear to George Washington that he wanted to be a justice of the Supreme Court or the secretary of the treasury, but the president never named him to any post.

Deane's reputation also spiraled downward. The attacks in Congress left him disillusioned about American democracy, and he returned to France in 1780. "We ought to inquire if any country ever was, for any time, even for one century at peace, free, and happy under a democracy," Deane wrote. British spies got their hands on this and other letters expressing similar sentiments and, recognizing their propaganda value, leaked them to American loyalists. The letters soon appeared in a New York newspaper, *The Royal Gazette*.

Deane pointed out these were his private letters, not meant for publication, and he also claimed the British had doctored them. But he didn't deny he had lost faith in the Revolution. "You believe that the peace, liberty, and happiness of our country will be best secured…under an independent democracy," he wrote Franklin. "I have the misfortune to think differently."

GEORGE WASHINGTON

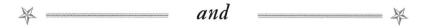 *and*

HARRY WASHINGTON

I do hereby...declare all indentured servants, Negroes, or others (appertaining to rebels), free that are able and willing to bear arms, they joining His Majesty's troops as soon as may be, for the more speedily reducing this colony to a proper sense of their duty.

LORD DUNMORE, VIRGINIA'S ROYAL GOVERNOR

AS MUCH AS DEANE AND LEE DETESTED EACH OTHER, NEITHER accused the other of fighting for the British. But there were plenty of Americans who did, including many slaves. These included Harry Washington, who took his master's surname and cared for George Washington's horses at the latter's Mount Vernon estate.

Harry was born in Africa around 1740 and sold into slavery somewhere near the Gambia River. After George bought him, he put Harry to work draining the Great Dismal Swamp, where George hoped to create a rice plantation. In 1771, Harry ran away but was captured.

The Revolution offered Harry another chance for freedom. Faced with a growing rebellion in Virginia, in November 1775 the colony's royal governor, Lord Dunmore, offered freedom to any slave willing to join the British forces.

Dunmore's emancipation proclamation realized the greatest fears of the rebels. It underlined the fact that many of those loudly demanding freedom were slaveholders, and it meant that many of those slaves might soon be armed against them.

The commander in chief of the American forces fully understood the danger Dunmore posed. "If…that man is not crushed before spring," George Washington wrote, "he will become the most formidable enemy America has—his strength will increase as a snowball by rolling; and faster, if some expedient cannot be hit upon to convince the slaves and servants of the impotency of his designs."

Washington also worried about his own slaves. His cousin and overseer Lund Washington reported from Mount Vernon that "there is not a man of them, but would leave us, if they believed they could make their escape." Lund added in explanation: "Liberty is sweet."

In the summer of 1776, soon after Congress had voted for independence, one of Dunmore's ships sailed up the Potomac River to Mount Vernon. When seventeen of Washington's slaves took the opportunity to join the British, Harry was among them.

Harry joined a group known as the Black Pioneers, went to New York with Dunmore at the end of 1776, and became a corporal in the Royal Artillery Department. The Black Pioneers moved south to fight various battles in the Carolina low country. When the British General Charles Cornwallis decided to move his troops into Virginia, he left a small garrison behind in Charleston, including Harry.

This was fortunate for Harry. In Virginia, Washington's troops besieged Cornwallis at Yorktown. With supplies running out, Cornwallis ordered the former slaves who had joined or accompanied his army out of the British camp. Most were captured by the Americans and returned to their former owners.

How many black men escaped and joined the British is a source of much debate among historians; estimates range from twenty thousand to one hundred thousand. In 1779, the British commander in chief Henry Clinton extended Dunmore's proclamation beyond Virginia and offered freedom to any slave of any rebellious American.

Washington, in contrast, was appalled to find blacks and whites serving side by side in the Continental Army. In October 1775, soon after he took command, he ordered a stop to the enlisting of black men. The idea of arming them scared all slave owners, and George owned many: in 1774 he owned 135 people, and the number increased during the war. But with recruitment a major problem, George realized he needed any soldiers he could get, and in December he reversed his position, allowing free black men (but not slaves) to enlist.

Exactly how many black men served on the patriot side is also uncertain. It was probably around five thousand—certainly many fewer than fought for the British—but George used them effectively. At Yorktown, where Cornwallis abandoned his black soldiers and followers, black patriots played a key role in capturing strategic positions.

Cornwallis's surrender at Yorktown essentially ended the Revolutionary War, leaving Harry stranded in Charleston. When the British evacuated Charleston in December 1782, many escaped slaves clung to the sides of the ships or tried to paddle alongside them in small boats. Harry was again fortunate—he boarded a British warship as a British soldier.

Harry landed in New York City, which was still under British control while the two sides negotiated a peace treaty in Paris. But the treaty, which was ratified in 1783, stated that the British would withdraw all its forces from the United States "without…carrying away any Negroes, or other property of the American inhabitants." Slave owners and their agents soon began arriving in New York to reclaim their property. George was about seventy miles up the Hudson River, preparing to negotiate the British departure from New York and well aware that "several of my own [slaves] are with the enemy."

Yet again Harry was fortunate, this time because the negotiator on the British side was Sir Guy Carleton, who commanded the remaining British forces in America. On May 6, Carleton met with George. Notes from the meeting indicate that Washington pressed Carleton for "the delivery of all Negroes and other property."

Carleton informed Washington that British troops were already in the process of evacuating New York and that "upwards of 6,000 persons…had embarked and sailed and that in this embarkation a number of Negroes were comprised." Washington was indignant, noting the treaty included "what appeared to him an express stipulation to the contrary." Carleton argued that the treaty applied only to Negroes who were currently American property and not to those the British had freed. "It could not have been the intention of the British government," Carleton insisted, "to reduce themselves to the necessity of violating their faith to the Negroes who came into the British lines under the proclamation of his predecessors in command."

Carleton's interpretation of the treaty's intent was certainly questionable, but his ultimate argument was moral and not legal. "Delivering up the Negroes to their former masters," he told Washington, "would be delivering them up some possibly to execution and others to severe punishment." This, in Carleton's opinion, would be "dishonorable."

In subsequent letters, George continued to press for the return of escaped slaves and Carleton continued to resist. Meanwhile, black people continued to board British ships bound for England, Jamaica, the Bahamas, and Nova Scotia. The British kept a record of all who departed, in part so that slave owners could be compensated. This was known as the "Book of Negroes." The listing of those who departed for Nova Scotia aboard *L'Abondance* on July 31, 1783, included "Harry Washington, 43, [fine] fellow. [Formerly the property] of General Washington; left him 7 [years ago]."

GEORGE'S VIEW OF BLACK PEOPLE AND SLAVERY CONTINUED TO evolve after the war. His will, drawn up in 1799, freed all the slaves held under his name and included provisions for feeding and clothing the elderly and educating the young among them. This did not place George in the forefront of the abolitionist movement, but it distinguished him from most other slaveholding founders.

"By freeing his slaves," biographer Ron Chernow wrote, "Washington accomplished something more glorious than any battlefield victory as a general or legislative act as president… He brought the American experience that much closer to the ideals of the American Revolution and brought his own behavior in line with his troubled conscience."

By the year of George's will and death, Harry had already been free for twenty-three years. Nova Scotia, however, did not turn out to be the Promised Land. Land and supplies promised by the British were slow to arrive. Both the rocky coast and many of its white inhabitants were inhospitable, and many black people lived in tents, despite the cold.

Harry fared better than many, acquiring two lots, a house, and forty acres. Nonetheless, in 1792, he joined more than a thousand other Nova Scotia settlers in a further exodus, this time back across the Atlantic. In Sierra Leone, on the west coast of Africa, they joined a small colony of former slaves. The outpost was perhaps five hundred miles from where Harry had been sold into slavery. Harry bought a farm east of Freetown and grew crops such as coffee, pepper, ginger, rice, cassava, and yams. The company that sponsored the Sierra Leone settlement managed it under the auspices of the British government. When the company demanded a payment from landowners like Harry, the colonists responded much as George and his counterparts had to British taxes: they sent a petition to King George, and they rallied behind their own elected officials. The company sent a new governor, Thomas Ludham, who was white, and refused to recognize the authority of any of the elected black legislators or judges.

In 1800, some of the colonists declared independence. Harry, like George before him, joined the rebels. But the British quelled this rebellion. Some of the rebels were hanged. Others, including Harry, were banished from the colony. At the age of sixty, Harry crossed the Sierra Leone River into exile. When and where he died is unknown, but it was as a free man.

BENJAMIN LINCOLN

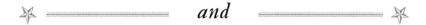

and

DANIEL SHAYS

Your resources are few, your force is inconsiderable, and hourly decreasing... You cannot hesitate a moment, to disband your deluded followers.

BENJAMIN LINCOLN TO DANIEL SHAYS

SEVEN MONTHS BEFORE GEORGE WASHINGTON'S TROOPS effectively ended the Revolutionary War with their 1781 victory at Yorktown, the Articles of Confederation went into effect. The Articles, drafted by John Dickinson, were America's first constitution. They established a very limited central government, which was understandable, given that Americans had rebelled against a powerful king and saw themselves as citizens of thirteen independent states.

The limitations of the Articles of Confederation were fully evident in 1786 and 1787 during what came to be known as Shays's Rebellion, after Daniel Shays. American history textbooks have traditionally and unfairly portrayed the uprising as little more than a warning sign for the new nation. Shays, the story goes, was an ambitious demagogue who manipulated some uneducated Massachusetts farmers who didn't want to pay their debts or their taxes. The rebellion was quickly suppressed by patriot militia led by the Revolutionary War hero Benjamin Lincoln. Most importantly, the rebellion also drove home the need for a stronger federal government, one capable of funding troops to put down an uprising.

After Shays's Rebellion, Revolutionary leaders quickly gathered in Philadelphia to replace the Articles of Confederation with a new constitution. "When rightly understood," George Richards Minot wrote in 1788, the history of the insurrections "does honor to the government, and displays the strongest marks of reflection and wisdom in the people."

Fuller histories of Shays's Rebellion reveal a more complex story. Daniel Shays and Benjamin Lincoln were both Revolutionary War officers, but they had very different ideas of what the Revolution meant.

NEITHER LINCOLN NOR SHAYS WOULD TOP MOST PEOPLE'S LIST OF founding fathers. But the Revolution was won and the new nation shaped by many—including African Americans and women—who make for a much more diverse portrait than the usual icons. Many of these founders, such as Shays, were not wealthy.

Shays fought at Lexington and at Bunker Hill. He commanded a militia unit at Saratoga and was a captain when he resigned his commission in 1780 and moved to the town of Pelham, about seventy miles west of Boston.

Like many farmers, Shays wound up in debt. Minot was quick to blame "this disposition of the people to indulge the use of luxuries." Falling prices and the scarcity of money were bigger problems, not only in Massachusetts but also across the new nation. In Massachusetts, the farmers' problems were exacerbated by the legislature, which in March 1785 decided to pay off its heavy war debt and also the state's share of the continental debt by raising taxes. Other states chose to pay their creditors only the much-depreciated value of the notes. Massachusetts chose to pay the full face value, which rewarded wealthy speculators who had bought the notes, often from poor farmers and veterans.

Even Minot, who in his 1788 history of the insurrections in Massachusetts often blamed the farmers for their plight, sympathized with those who had "shed their blood in the field, to be worn out with burdensome taxes at home; or…to secure to their creditors, a right to drag them into courts and prisons." Shays's debt forced him to sell a sword that he had been given by the Marquis de Lafayette.

In September 1786, protesters "headed by one Daniel Shays" (Minot reported) occupied the Hampshire County courthouse, where they faced militiamen under the command of Major General William Shepard. The standoff lasted three days, after which the judges decided it was hopeless to try to conduct court business. No shots were fired.

The protests in Hampshire and other western Massachusetts counties spooked Governor James Bowdoin and the legislature. On January 4, 1787, Bowdoin called for raising an army to be commanded by Benjamin Lincoln.

Lincoln's service in the Revolution was more famous than Shays's, but also more checkered. Like Shays, Lincoln had fought heroically at Saratoga. But in Charleston, where Lincoln commanded all American forces, he had surrendered his entire army to the British. After an exchange of prisoners, Lincoln joined George Washington's forces in Virginia. He gained some measure of revenge for the defeat at Charleston when the British surrendered at Yorktown and Washington designated him to receive the sword of the British commander.

Whatever his merits as a military commander, Lincoln was politically in step with Bowdoin and the Massachusetts legislature. He was himself a holder of government notes to be paid off by the new taxes, and he shared the views of many in the Boston elite about the western farmers and their protests. "People were diverted from their usual industry and economy," he explained to Washington. "A luxuriant mode of living crept into vogue, and soon that income, by which the expenses of all should as much as possible be limited, was no longer considered as having anything to do with the question at what expense families ought to live."

With Lincoln's army approaching, Shays realized his own forces would need more arms and ammunition. On January 25, 1787, Shays led an attack on the federal arsenal at Springfield. Shepard again commanded the government troops. This time, shots were fired, killing four farmers and wounding several others. Shays and his followers fled north in disarray.

Lincoln arrived in Springfield on January 27 and quickly set off in pursuit of Shays. On the thirtieth, Lincoln sent Shays a message calling for his surrender:

> *Your resources are few, your force is inconsiderable, and hourly decreasing from the disaffection of your men. You are in a post where you have neither cover nor supplies, and in a situation in which you can neither give aid to your friends, nor discomfort to the supporters of good order and government. Under these circumstances, you cannot hesitate a moment, to disband your deluded followers.*

Shays answered that he and his men would lay down their arms in return for a general pardon. The next day Shays offered a cease-fire if the legislature would consider an "accommodation of our present unhappy affairs."

Lincoln rejected Shays's offers. Instead, Lincoln marched his troops thirty miles through a blizzard and attacked. Surprised, more than a hundred of the rebels surrendered. The rest fled. Some took refuge in Vermont, New Hampshire, and New York, while a few continued to carry out occasional attacks. But the rebellion was essentially over.

The most pressing question was now: how ought the vanquished rebels be punished?

The legislators in Boston could not help but remember that, only a few years earlier, many of them had taken up arms against a government they considered oppressive. But Great Britain was a monarchy, and Massachusetts was a republic. "In monarchies," explained Samuel Adams, "the crime of treason and rebellion may admit of being pardoned or lightly punished; but the man who dares to rebel against the laws of a republic ought to suffer death."

Lincoln was more forgiving. He urged leniency for most of the rebels but suggested that "a few prompt examples" be made of the leaders.

The authorities in Boston took Lincoln's approach. They stripped the rebels of their citizenship but provided a path to a pardon for those who would sign an oath of loyalty. Shays, still on the loose in Vermont, was found guilty of treason (a verdict in absentia) and condemned to hang.

Massachusetts voters were even more forgiving than Lincoln. Hoping to put the rebellion behind them, they elected a new legislature and replaced Bowdoin with his predecessor, John Hancock. The new legislators and governor provided much of the tax relief the rebels had wanted, and Hancock pardoned Shays.

Lincoln emerged from the rebellion a hero. His victory over Shays eclipsed his surrender at Charleston. He basked in the praise of, among others, Washington, who congratulated him on "the suppression of those tumults and insurrections with so little blood shed" and called this "an event as happy as it was unexpected." When Washington was elected president, he appointed Lincoln as head of the Boston Customs office.

Shays's future was less secure. Though pardoned, he never returned to Massachusetts. And the authorities in Boston still demonized him as the man who led—or rather misled—the "deluded" farmers. He was called a tool of the British, a would-be dictator, a "generalissimo." Shays denied he was even the leader of the rebellion. "I at their head! I am not," he exclaimed to General Rufus Putnam, who reported the interview to Governor Bowdoin. "I never had any appointment but that at Springfield, nor did I ever take command of any men but those of the county of Hampshire;… I never had half so much to do with the matter as you think."

Shays was not trying to avoid responsibility; the rebellion had no single leader. Indeed, the rebels' defeat at Springfield was in large part due to their lack of organization of any sort.

Even the name of the uprising—Shays's Rebellion—was misleading. The rebels referred to themselves not as Shaysites but as "Regulators," since their aim was to regulate the abuses of the government. By naming the rebellion after Shays, its opponents downplayed the extent to which it was a genuinely populist uprising.

The textbook histories, too, were too quick to reduce the uprising to a mere warning sign about the need for a stronger federal government. True, the rebellion did spur calls for a new constitution. And true, Article 1, Section 8 of the Constitution would give the federal government the power to "suppress insurrections." But the rebellion was every bit as much an expression of "We the People" as was the Constitution that followed from it.

PATRICK HENRY

and

JAMES MADISON

I smelt a rat.

PATRICK HENRY

SHAYS'S REBELLION WAS HARDLY THE ONLY SIGN OF WEAKNESS IN THE Articles of Confederation. These United States were barely united. They were unable to agree on either foreign or domestic policy, or how to deal with the postwar depression. In May 1787, delegates from twelve states (Rhode Island sent none) arrived in Philadelphia to define a new federal government. In September, they had a new constitution.

For the Constitution to become the law of the land, conventions in nine states had to ratify it. By June 1788, eight states had done so. Anti-Federalists, as opponents of the new Constitution came to be called, saw the Virginia ratifying convention of June 1788 as their last stand.

The leading Anti-Federalist in Virginia was Patrick Henry, who was generally acknowledged as the Revolution's greatest orator. The leading Federalist in Virginia, indeed in all the United States, was James Madison, generally acknowledged as the founder most responsible for the Constitution.

"Even more than the Lincoln-Douglas debate over slavery, or the Darrow-Bryan debate over evolution," wrote historian Joseph Ellis, "the Henry-Madison debate in June of 1788 can lay plausible claim to being the most consequential debate in American history."

❖◆◗◖◆❖

William Wirt, in his 1817 biography of Patrick Henry, described how the twenty-nine-year-old delegate addressed the Virginia House of Burgesses in May 1765 to protest the Stamp Act. Wirt described how Henry, "in a voice of thunder, and with the look of a god," declared that "Caesar had his Brutus—Charles the First, his Cromwell—and George the Third…*may profit by their example.*" Interrupted by cries of "Treason," Henry responded, "If this be treason, make the most of it."

Among those who witnessed Henry's speech in Williamsburg was Thomas Jefferson, then a twenty-two-year-old law student and later Madison's close friend and political ally. Jefferson admired the power of Henry's oratory, but he despised the man. "His imagination was copious, poetical, sublime," Jefferson wrote, "but vague also. He said the strongest things in the finest language, but without logic, without arrangement, desultorily." More bluntly, Jefferson described Henry as "all tongue without either head or heart."

In 1777 Henry clashed with Jefferson—and Madison—over

the relationship between church and state. Henry wanted people to pay taxes to support a church of their choice. Compared to having an official state church, as the Virginia colony once had, this was certainly a step toward freedom of religion. Jefferson and Madison wanted a more complete separation of church and state; they argued that churches did not need and should not receive any taxpayer money. Jefferson drafted a "bill for establishing religious freedom" in 1777. In 1785, by which time Jefferson was in France serving as America's ambassador, Madison managed to push aside Henry's proposal for taxes to support churches and push through the Assembly a revised version of Jefferson's bill.

Despite being outmaneuvered on the church-state issue, Henry wielded great power in the Virginia legislature. He successfully blocked efforts by Jefferson and Madison to revise Virginia's 1776 constitution. From Paris, a frustrated Jefferson wrote Madison: "While Mr. Henry lives, another bad constitution would be formed, and saddled forever on us. What we have to do I think is devoutly to pray for his death."

The fight over Virginia's constitution foreshadowed the battle over the new federal constitution. For Madison, the flaws of Virginia's constitution paled beside those of the Articles of Confederation, and those flaws prompted Madison to take the lead in creating the new U.S. Constitution.

"You give me a credit to which I have no claim," Madison later wrote, "in calling me 'The writer of the Constitution of the U.S.'... It ought to be regarded as the work of many heads and many hands."

But there was no question that Madison influenced the document more than anyone else.

Madison also led the fight for its ratification. Along with Alexander Hamilton and John Jay, he published a series of essays defending the Constitution. Jefferson described the *Federalist*, as the essays were called, as "the best commentary on the principles of government which ever was written."

Henry was among those the Virginia Assembly selected to attend the constitutional convention in Philadelphia with Madison. He declined. "I smelt a rat," Henry reportedly said. Madison hoped he might bring him around, and George Washington wrote Henry that the Constitution was "the best that could be obtained at this time."

Henry quickly squelched their hopes. "I have to lament that I cannot bring my mind to accord with the proposed constitution," he replied to Washington. "The concern I feel on this account is really greater than I am able to express."

Henry had no problem expressing his concerns when the Virginia ratifying convention convened in Richmond. His opening speech made clear the stakes. "I conceive the Republic to be in extreme danger," he exclaimed. "If a wrong step be now made, the Republic may be lost forever. If this new government will not come up to the expectation of the people…their liberty will be lost, and tyranny must and will arise."

Henry challenged the premise of the Constitution's opening words. "What right had they to say, *We, the People*?" he asked of the

Philadelphia delegates. "Who authorized them to speak the language of, *We, the People*, instead of *We, the States*?... The people gave them no power to use their name."

The delegates had been sent to Philadelphia, he stressed, to amend the Articles of Confederation, not to create an entirely new constitution. Nor was there any *need* for a new constitution. There was no crisis, Henry insisted, at least in Virginia: "Disorders have arisen in other parts of America, but here, sir, no dangers, no insurrection or tumult, has happened—everything has been calm and tranquil."

Madison could not match Henry's passion—in fact, the convention's stenographer complained Madison spoke so quietly he could barely be heard—but he was logical and systematic. He repeated many of the arguments set forth in the *Federalist*, stressing that the powers of the new federal government would be limited by the states and that the power of the president would be checked and balanced by the powers of Congress and the courts. "The powers of the federal government are enumerated," he explained. "It can only operate in certain cases."

Henry did not buy it. Again and again he rose to speak; over the course of the three and a half weeks the delegates met, Henry spoke nearly one-quarter of the time.

He reminded his fellow Virginians of his stance against the Stamp Act: "Twenty-three years ago was I supposed a traitor to my country," he said. "I may be thought suspicious when I say our privileges and rights are in danger... But, sir, suspicion is a virtue, as long as its object is the preservation of the public good."

Henry suspected that at least some of those behind the Constitution had an ulterior motive. "When the American spirit was in its youth…liberty…was then the primary object," he said. "But now…the American spirit…is about to convert this country [in]to a powerful and mighty empire… There will be no checks, no real balances, in this government."

In his final speech at the ratifying convention, Henry extended the stakes beyond America to the world; indeed, the heavens:

He [Madison] tells you of important blessings which he imagines will result to us and mankind in general, from the adoption of this system—I see the awful immensity of the dangers with which it is pregnant.—I see it—I feel it.—I see beings of a higher order, anxious concerning our decision. When I see beyond the horizon that binds human eyes, and look at the final consummation of all human things, and see those intelligent beings which inhabit the ethereal mansions, reviewing the political decisions and revolutions which in the progress of time will happen in America, and the consequent happiness or misery of mankind—I am led to believe that much of the account on one side or the other will depend on what we now decide.

At about this point, the stenographer noted, "a violent storm arose, which put the house in such disorder, that Mr. Henry was obliged to conclude." Archibald Stuart, a delegate to the ratifying convention, described Henry as "rising on the wings of the tempest, to seize upon the artillery of heaven, and direct its fiercest thunders against the heads of his adversaries."

The artillery of heaven was not enough. The next day, June 25, the convention voted 89–79 to ratify the Constitution.

———◆◆◆———

HENRY TOOK SOME SATISFACTION IN THE FACT THAT THE ratifying convention recommended forty amendments to the Constitution. These were not binding, since Virginians could not force other states to go along with them. But the ratifying convention's recommendations surely added to the pressure to amend the Constitution.

Henry also gained some revenge later that year, when the Virginia Assembly chose the commonwealth's first two senators. Madison finished third in the voting, behind two Anti-Federalists backed by Henry. Madison managed to win a seat in the House of Representatives, despite Henry's support for his opponent, the Anti-Federalist James Monroe. (This was the first and last time that two future presidents would run against each other for a seat in Congress.) During the campaign, Madison promised he would support amending the Constitution, and once elected he did just that—introducing the amendments that would eventually become the Bill of Rights and that would guarantee, among other rights, freedom of religion, speech, press, and assembly.

By 1791, Henry had reconciled himself to the Constitution. "Although the form of government into which my country-men determined to place themselves had my enmity," he wrote Monroe, "yet as we are one and all embarked, it is natural to care for the crazy machine, at least so long as we are out of sight of a port to refit." By 1795, Washington was so convinced of Henry's loyalty that the president asked him to become secretary of state. Henry declined. He had, he explained, eight children by his current marriage, and his finances and health were precarious. But, Henry emphasized, "I have bid adieu to the distinction of federal and antifederal ever since the commencement of the present government, and in the circle of my friends have often expressed my fears of disunion amongst the states."

Jefferson and Madison, meanwhile, were increasingly worried about the power of the federal government and found themselves making some of the same arguments Henry had made for states' rights. The Republican Party they eventually founded cannot be defined as simply the successor to Anti-Federalism; the evolution of both the Federalist and Republican parties was more complicated than that. But there is no doubt that Madison's embrace of Henry's arguments is, as Ellis put it, "one of the richest ironies in American history."

As for Jefferson, his fears about the power of the federal government would be tightly linked to his fears about the man who would try to wield those powers: Alexander Hamilton.

ALEXANDER HAMILTON

 *and*

THOMAS JEFFERSON

A man whose history...is a tissue of machinations against the liberty of the country.

THOMAS JEFFERSON ON ALEXANDER HAMILTON

If...the people of the United States [for] national union, national respectability, public order, and public credit... are willing to substitute national disunion, national insignificance, public disorder, and discredit...let him be the toast of every political club and the theme of every popular huzza.

ALEXANDER HAMILTON ON THOMAS JEFFERSON

IN RETIREMENT AT MONTICELLO, THOMAS JEFFERSON REMINISCED about a dinner party that had taken place when he was George Washington's secretary of state. Jefferson invited Vice President John Adams and Treasury Secretary Alexander Hamilton. After dinner and over wine, Adams and Hamilton discussed the merits of the British system of government. According to Jefferson, Adams said that "if some of its defects and abuses were corrected," Britain's was "the most perfect constitution of government ever devised by man." Hamilton went further, saying that even "with its existing vices, it was the most perfect model of government that could be formed; and that the correction of its vices would render it an impracticable government."

That same evening, Hamilton asked about three portraits hanging on Jefferson's walls. Jefferson identified the subjects as Francis Bacon, Isaac Newton, and John Locke, "my trinity of the three greatest men the world had ever produced." Hamilton responded (this still according to Jefferson), "The greatest man…that ever lived was Julius Caesar."

With these anecdotes, Jefferson condensed his version of the political philosophies of his two greatest opponents. Adams was at best wavering in his support of the Republic. Hamilton was much worse: given the opportunity, he would discard the Constitution and replace it with a government more tyrannical than that against which Americans had fought the Revolution.

Hamilton's view of Jefferson was equally derogatory: he was a hypocrite, talking of liberty while holding slaves; he was a naïve philosopher easily seduced by the radical ideas that had swept through France after its Revolution and threatened to bring the same terror to America. The greatest danger to the republic, Hamilton believed, was the chaos that would ensue if Jefferson had his way. Unchecked, the revolution would degenerate into mob rule. "Tired at length of anarchy, or want of government," Hamilton wrote in 1792, Americans might then "take shelter in the arms of monarchy."

———◆◆◆———

THERE WAS CERTAINLY AN IRONY TO JEFFERSON'S VIEW THAT HE was the champion of the oppressed and Hamilton of the wealthy. Jefferson was born to luxury. Hamilton, an illegitimate child whose mother died when he was thirteen, was largely self-taught and self-made. And while Jefferson's authorship of the Declaration of Independence was an incomparable contribution to the Revolution, it was Hamilton who fought in the war. It was Hamilton who suffered through a winter at Valley Forge, who was injured at the Battle of Monmouth, who led a crucial charge at Yorktown. Jefferson spent much of the war at home, and when British forces approached Monticello, he fled. "The governor of the ancient dominion," Hamilton later wrote, "dwindled into the poor, timid philosopher, and instead of rallying his brave countrymen, he fled for safety from a few light horsemen and shamefully abandoned his trust." This was unfair: Jefferson's retreat was undoubtedly prudent. Still, it was hardly heroic.

Hamilton had also played a far larger role than Jefferson in securing the ratification of the Constitution. *The Federalist*, first published in newspapers and then as a book, set forth the case for replacing the Articles of Confederation with a stronger national government. James Madison wrote twenty-nine of these essays and

John Jay five; Hamilton wrote eighty-five. Jefferson, concerned about the proposed constitution's lack of a bill of rights and busy as an American minister to France, largely stayed out of the ratification fight.

Hamilton and Jefferson may have met in 1783, but they did not come to know each other until Washington appointed Hamilton as his secretary of the treasury and Jefferson as his secretary of state. They quickly came to know each other all too well. Their first major disagreement was over Hamilton's plan for the federal government to pay off the debts of the state by borrowing more money. Hamilton saw this as a way to strengthen the new federal government, because it would not only establish it as worthy of credit, but also necessitate federal taxes to pay off the debts. However, Jefferson saw this as a way to reward wealthy speculators in government securities at the expense of the original holders of the securities, many of whom were veterans of the Revolution. Jefferson also noted that Virginia was one of four states that had already paid off its Revolutionary debts, and he saw no reason for Virginians to pay taxes to pay off others' debts. At the very least, Virginia ought to get something in return.

And so to another dinner, again hosted and again described by Jefferson. This time Jefferson's guests were Hamilton and Madison, and the conversation turned to Virginians' objections to Hamilton's plan. "I was persuaded that men of sound heads and honest views needed nothing more than explanation and mutual understanding to enable them to unite in some measures which might enable us to get along," Jefferson later wrote. "It was observed, I forget by which of them, that as the pill would be a bitter one to the southern states, something should be done to soothe them."

What soothed the Southerners was a deal to locate the capital of the United States not in Philadelphia or New York but at a new city to be built along the Potomac River, not far from Mount Vernon. Madison agreed to sell the deal to Southerners; they would get the capital in the South. Hamilton agreed to sell the deal to Northerners; they would get the tax plan they wanted. In July 1790, the House agreed both to the federal assumption of state debts and to locate the capital at what would become Washington, DC.

The "mutual understanding" between Hamilton and Jefferson would not last long.

HAMILTON'S PLANS FOR EXPANDING THE SCOPE OF THE FEDERAL GOVernment went beyond assuming state debts. Next up on his agenda was a central bank, which would be partly capitalized by the government and would issue currency to be used throughout the nation. Hamilton's plans also included federal subsidies for manufacturers and national defense contracts. He thought all this crucial for building the economy, and he was right. But an economy based on manufacturing and trade and centered in Northern cities was a very different economy—indeed, a very different America— than the agrarian republic Jefferson envisioned. The economic transformation Hamilton sought was as much of a revolution as the political one defined by Jefferson's Declaration.

The public, Hamilton believed, would understand that "their happiness and their safety are connected with the existence and maintenance of an efficient national or federal government." Jefferson saw a more sinister design. Hamilton's economic program was "an engine in the hands of the executive branch of government, which added to the great patronage it possessed...might enable it to assume by degrees a kingly authority." Hamilton's ultimate object was a change "from the present republican form of government to that of a monarchy."

Hamilton flatly denied the charge: "The idea of introducing a monarchy or aristocracy into this country," he wrote, "is one...that none but madmen could meditate."

Jefferson argued that the Constitution did not authorize the government to create a bank. Hamilton argued that to limit the government powers to those explicitly spelled out in the Constitution would be to "furnish the singular spectacle of a political society without sovereignty, or of a people governed without government."

Washington generally sided with Hamilton; he signed the bank bill into law in February 1791. Jefferson, increasingly frustrated, concealed neither his sense of his own superiority nor his contempt for Hamilton. He told Washington he could not "suffer...the slanders of a man whose history, from the moment at which history can stoop to notice him, is a tissue of machinations against the liberty of the country which has not only received and given him bread, but heaped its honors on his head."

Unable to sway the president, Jefferson took the fight to the press. The problem was the nation's most influential newspaper, the *Gazette of the United States*, supported Hamilton's position. So Jefferson took matters into his own hands and recruited Philip Freneau to publish a rival newspaper, the *National Gazette*. He even gave Freneau a job in the State Department to supplement his income. Hamilton wasn't going to delegate his case to anyone; he himself wrote in the *Gazette of the United States* that Jefferson's principles would result in a "national government transformed into the skeleton of power" and that his politics "have ever aimed at depressing the national authority."

The debates over economic policy were exacerbated by those over foreign policy. Most Americans supported the French Revolution, at first. After all, the French had supported the American Revolution, and the French revolutionaries trumpeted the words of Americans like Jefferson and Thomas Paine. But by 1793, it was clear that the Revolution in France threatened the social and economic order there. Hamilton and many other Americans were frightened and appalled by "ruin and devastation far and wide—subverting the foundations of right security and property, of order, morality and religion." Jefferson, of course, had a different perspective. Liberties had to be fought for, and that meant blood had to be shed.

"Of all the events that shaped the political life of the new Republic," historians Stanley Elkins and Eric McKitrick wrote, "none was more central than the massive personal and political enmity...which developed in the course of the 1790s between Alexander Hamilton and Thomas Jefferson."

Hamilton and Jefferson were, the latter later recalled, "daily pitted in the cabinet like two cocks." Washington tried to mediate. "I believe the views of both of you are pure, and well meant," he told Jefferson. Washington's efforts were in vain. At the end of 1793, Jefferson resigned from the cabinet and became the leader of America's first opposition party.

THE 1796 ELECTION FORCED HAMILTON TO CHOOSE BETWEEN Adams, the Federalist candidate, and Jefferson, the Republican. Hamilton was no fan of Adams but thought him far better than the alternative. "All personal and partial considerations must be discarded," he wrote as the election approached, "and everything must give way to the great object of excluding Jefferson."

After Adams won, Jefferson continued in opposition, with the nation increasingly polarized. "The passions are too high at present to be cooled," Jefferson wrote in 1797.

In their 1800 rematch, Jefferson defeated Adams. But, because the Constitution did not then make a distinction between votes for president and vice president, Jefferson ended up with the same number of electoral votes as Aaron Burr, even though most Republicans thought of Burr as their vice-presidential candidate. This threw the election into the House of Representatives, where many Federalists thought Burr was the better choice. They figured since Burr was from New York, he would better understand northern commercial interests.

Hamilton despised Jefferson, yet he despised Burr even more. Jefferson, he explained, at least had "pretensions to character." Hamilton was no longer as influential as he once was, but he still mattered, and the House ultimately chose Jefferson.

Hamilton was right to suspect that, in some senses, a Jefferson presidency would not be as radical as Jefferson's rhetoric. Even Jefferson's rhetoric quickly softened. His inaugural address was conciliatory. "Every difference of opinion is not a difference of principle," he proclaimed. "We are all Republicans: we are all Federalists."

Jefferson did not get rid of Hamilton's bank, nor did he lead America into war against England for the sake of France. More fundamentally, as president he made no effort to dismantle the federal government.

Was Hamilton, then, the "winner" of his feud with Jefferson? Yes and no.

The America that evolved after their deaths—urban and industrial, expansive, inclusive, and powerful—was very much Hamilton's.

But Jefferson's presidency was truly revolutionary. Suffrage rights were broadened, and though of course they still excluded women and African Americans, this was nonetheless a step toward a more inclusive democracy. Later generations of Americans would go much further, inspired by Jefferson's words. It's Jefferson's monument that stands on the mall in Washington, and it's his words we remember.

JOHN ADAMS

and

THOMAS JEFFERSON

That you and I differ in our ideas of the best form of government is well-known to us both.

THOMAS JEFFERSON TO JOHN ADAMS

His mind is now poisoned with passion, prejudice, and faction.

JOHN ADAMS ON THOMAS JEFFERSON

JOHN TRUMBULL'S ICONIC 1818 PAINTING *DECLARATION OF Independence* portrays the moment when the drafting committee presented the document to the Continental Congress. John Adams and Thomas Jefferson are most prominent in the painting, with Benjamin Franklin off to the side and the other two members of the committee behind them.

It's doubtful the committee actually stood like this, but Trumbull's placement was certainly appropriate. No one had argued for independence longer and more vociferously than

Adams, so much so that he readily admitted his fellow congressmen considered him "obnoxious." And no one but Jefferson could have expressed the case for independence so eloquently.

They were, as historian Joseph Ellis wrote, "the odd couple of the American Revolution." Adams was short and fat, Jefferson tall and thin. Adams was a northerner, Jefferson a southerner. Adams had made himself unpopular by arguing nonstop; Jefferson rarely spoke in Congress, preferring to express himself in writing. Together, they did more for the Revolution than anyone, except possibly Franklin and George Washington.

The Adams-Jefferson partnership extended well beyond 1776 and included a variety of diplomatic assignments in Europe. When Jefferson joined him in Paris, Adams was delighted. "My new partner is an old friend," he wrote. "I am very happy in him." And when Adams left France to become America's ambassador to Great Britain, his wife, Abigail, regretted having "to leave behind me the only person with whom my companion could associate with perfect freedom, and unreserve."

Jefferson was equally enamored. He conceded that Adams was "vain" and "irritable," but he insisted to James Madison that Adams was "as disinterested as the being which made him [and]… so amiable, that I pronounce you will love him if ever you become acquainted with him."

Unlike Jefferson and Alexander Hamilton, who only reluctantly worked together before turning against each other, Jefferson and Adams were friends as well as collaborators. The widowed

Jefferson spent much time at the home of Abigail and John. When Jefferson's eight-year-old daughter arrived in London en route to join her father in Paris, she stayed with the Adamses, and Abigail was so sad to see little Polly leave for Paris that she admitted to Jefferson she was "tempted to have kept her arrival here, from you a secret."

WHAT TORE APART THE COLLABORATION AND THE FRIENDSHIP were the politics of Washington's administration, in which Adams served as vice president and Jefferson as secretary of state.

Adams, like most in what would become the Federalist Party, believed the best way to protect liberty was to invest power in a strong executive—one who could ignore political pressures and act on behalf of the public good. Adams believed the president should have a title commensurate with his authority and status, and in 1789 he was among those advocating for a title along the lines of "His Highness the President of the United States and Protector of the Rights of the Same."

This did not go over well in a nation that had not so long ago fought a revolution against a king. Jefferson, along with most of those in what would become the Republican Party, had more faith than Adams in the people's ability to govern themselves. Jefferson thought the proposed title for the president "the most superlatively ridiculous thing I ever heard of" and said it was proof that Franklin had been right to say of Adams: "Always an honest man, often a great one, but sometimes absolutely mad."

The excesses of the French Revolution brought to the fore Federalist fears about democracy. In a series of essays published in the *Gazette of the United States* in 1791, Adams set forth the case for monarchy. "Mankind found by experience, government necessary to the preservation of their lives, liberties, and properties," he wrote. "They had found so much diversity of opinion and sentiment among them…so many rivalries among the principal men, such divisions, confusions, and miseries, that they had almost unanimously been convinced that hereditary succession was attended with fewer evils than frequent elections."

Adams's essays were historical and philosophical; he did not want to turn Washington from a president into a king. But for Republicans, they were damning evidence that the vice president had abandoned the principles of the Revolution. Jefferson, on reading Thomas Paine's defense of the French Revolution, wrote to Jonathan B. Smith that he was pleased that it was to be reprinted in America and that "something is at length to be publicly said against the political heresies which have sprung up among us." When Jefferson's words to Smith appeared in the American edition of Paine's *Rights of Man*, Adams was furious.

Jefferson explained to Adams he had never intended his criticism to be public. "The friendship and confidence which has so long existed between us required this explanation from me, and I know you too well to fear any misconstruction of the motives of it," he wrote. But Jefferson could not paper over their philosophical differences, telling Adams, "That you and I differ in our ideas of the best form of government is well-known to us both."

On issue after issue, Washington sided with Adams (and his treasury secretary, Alexander Hamilton), and in December 1793, Jefferson resigned from the cabinet. The Adams-Jefferson partnership was over, and the friendship was frayed. "Jefferson went off yesterday, and good riddance," John wrote Abigail. "He has talents I know, and integrity I believe: but his mind is now poisoned with passion, prejudice, and faction."

After Washington announced he would not run for a third term, Adams and Jefferson vied to succeed him. In keeping with the customs of the period, they did not openly campaign, leaving it to others to work on their behalf. But there was no question both wanted the job.

Adams swept New England, Jefferson the South. That gave Adams 71 electoral votes and Jefferson 68. Given the Constitutional provisions then in effect, Adams would be president and Jefferson vice president.

Jefferson was prepared not only to concede defeat but also, in the spirit of national unity, to work with Adams. He drafted a letter in which he wished Adams an administration "filled with glory and happiness to yourself and advantage to us." He assured

Adams that, though "various little incidents have happened or been contrived to separate us," he retained "the solid esteem of the moments when we were working for our independence, and sentiments of respect and affectionate attachment."

Jefferson sent Madison the draft of the letter to Adams, explaining he could not object to taking a secondary position to Adams. "I am his junior in life, was his junior in Congress, his junior in the diplomatic line, his junior lately in our civil government," Jefferson wrote. If Adams could be convinced to give up his bias toward a government too much like a monarchy, he told Madison, Jefferson would be happy to support him now and in the future.

Madison urged Jefferson not to commit to anything that would hamper his ability to criticize Adams or to run against him again four years later. Explained Madison: "There may be real embarrassments from giving written possession to him, of the degree of compliment and confidence which your personal delicacy and friendship have suggested."

Jefferson bowed to Madison's political wisdom. He never sent the letter to Adams.

HAD JEFFERSON SENT THE LETTER, MIGHT THE INTENSE partisanship of the late 1790s have been avoided? Almost certainly not. Too many forces were pulling apart Federalists and Republicans—and Adams and Jefferson.

The undeclared Quasi-War with France, a series of naval engagements between 1798 and 1800, widened the gap between Francophobe Federalists and Francophile Republicans. Federalists feared the unfettered democracy of the French Revolution would eventually lead to tyranny—fears they saw realized with Napoleon Bonaparte's coup. Republicans feared Federalists would do away with democracy altogether—fears they saw as close to being realized when Adams both approved the creation of a standing army under the command of Alexander Hamilton and signed into law the Sedition Act, which Federalists used to prosecute newspaper editors who criticized the government.

"I consider these laws as merely an experiment on the American mind to see how far it will bear an avowed violation of the Constitution," Jefferson warned. He predicted that, if laws like the Sedition Act were allowed to stand, "we shall immediately see attempted another act of Congress declaring that the president shall continue in office during life, reserving to another occasion the transfer of the succession to his heirs, and the establishment of the Senate for life."

The election of 1800 was a rematch of 1796, with the stakes and rhetoric raised. Early in 1800, the Republican pamphleteer James Callender published the contemptuously anti-Adams *The Prospect before Us*. For Callender, the choice was "between Adams, war, and beggary, and Jefferson, peace, and competency."

For Federalists, the choice was equally clear. In New York, the *Daily Advertiser* broke it down this way:

You who are for French notions of government, for the tempes-
tuous sea of anarchy and misrule; for arming the poor against
the rich; for fraternizing with the foes of God and man; go
to the left and support the leaders, or the dupes of the anti-
federal junto. But you that are sober, industrious, thriving
and happy, give your votes for those men who mean to preserve
the union of these states; the purity and rigor of our excellent
Constitution; the sacred majesty of the laws; and the holy ordi-
nances of religion.

Federalists also attacked Jefferson for his alleged atheism. "The grand question," stated the *Gazette of the United States*, was: "Shall I continue in allegiance to God—and a religious president; or impiously declare for Jefferson—and no god!!!"

Despite the Federalists' efforts, between 1796 and 1800 the Republicans gained ground, especially among people who worked with their hands and saw the Federalists as the party of wealthy aristocrats. Jefferson ended up with 73 electoral votes, Adams 65.

Jefferson later referred to the election as "the revolution of 1800, for that was as real a revolution in the principles of our government as that of 1776 was in its form; not effected indeed by the sword, as that, but by the rational and peaceable instrument of reform, the suffrage of the people." The years following Jefferson's election did not fulfill the promise of Jefferson's Declaration: they did not treat all men, let alone women, as created equal. But for white men, the election was a big step toward a more democratic nation. And Jefferson was certainly correct to stress the revolutionary nature of a peaceful transfer of power. Despite the rhetoric on both sides, Americans in general accepted that democracy could survive—indeed, would flourish—with parties competing for power.

Adams might have taken some consolation in how close the election was. He did far better than Federalist candidates for Congress. Indeed, Adams would have been reelected, had the Constitution not counted each slave as three-fifths of a person when apportioning Electoral College votes (without, of course, letting slaves vote).

Adams did not attend Jefferson's inauguration. He left Washington early that morning and never returned.

For three years no words passed between Jefferson and either Adams, and then it was Abigail who broke the silence. The occasion was the death of Jefferson's daughter Polly in April 1804, soon after a difficult childbirth. Abigail, remembering how close she had been to Jefferson and to Polly, reached out to offer her condolences.

Jefferson replied with appreciation and assurances that the rivalry others saw between her husband and himself had not lessened their "mutual esteem." Jefferson added that only one act of Adams had given him "personal displeasure." This was Adams's appointment, in the last weeks of his administration, of Federalists to various judgeships. Among them was John Marshall, a long-time enemy of Jefferson, whom Adams had appointed chief justice of the Supreme Court.

Abigail was infuriated that Jefferson responded to her personal note with political criticism of her husband. She let loose her own deeply felt resentment of Jefferson's support of James Callender, whose newspaper attacks on Adams were "the lowest and vilest slander, which malice could invent." This was what "severed the bonds of former friendship," she said, "and placed you in a light very different from what I once viewed you in."

Callender had been jailed under the Sedition Act, but Jefferson pardoned him. When Jefferson wouldn't also pay his fine, Callender turned on the president and exposed in print Jefferson's sexual relationship with Sally Hemings, an enslaved woman at Monticello. Abigail could not resist gloating: "The serpent you cherished and warmed bit the hand that nourished him."

John did not know about Abigail's correspondence with Jefferson until it was over, and this might have been the end of the Adams-Jefferson relationship, had it not been for Benjamin Rush, a fellow signer of the Declaration of Independence. Rush took it upon himself to renew the friendship between Adams and Jefferson, suggesting to each that the other was ready for a reconciliation.

On January 1, 1812, Adams wrote Jefferson wishing him a happy new year and promising to send a gift of some yarn. Jefferson responded warmly:

A letter from you calls up recollections very dear to my mind. It carries me back to the times when, beset with difficulties and dangers, we were fellow laborers in the same cause, struggling for what is most valuable to man, his right of self-government. Laboring always at the same oar, with some wave ever ahead threatening to overwhelm us.

The two ex-presidents were soon writing each other regularly, discussing politics and history and philosophy as if their differences had never been personal. "As we had been longer than most others on the public theater," wrote Jefferson, "and our names therefore were more familiar to our countrymen, the party which considered you as thinking with them placed your name at their head; the other, for the same reason, selected mine."

"You and I ought not to die," Adams wrote, "before we have explained ourselves to each other." And explain they did, to each other and to posterity, over the course of 158 letters between 1812 and their deaths on July 4, 1826. That Adams and Jefferson died within hours of each other and on the fiftieth anniversary of the day Congress adopted the Declaration of Independence is a story often told, yet still incredible.

"We acted in perfect harmony through a long and perilous contest for our liberty and independence," Jefferson wrote. "A constitution has been acquired which, though neither of us think perfect, yet both consider as competent to render our fellow citizens the happiest and the securest on whom the sun has ever shone. If we do not think exactly alike as to its imperfections, it matters little to our country which, after devoting to it long lives of disinterested labor, we have delivered over to our successors in life, who will be able to take care of it, and of themselves."

JOHN ADAMS

and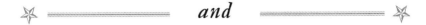

ALEXANDER HAMILTON

I have read his heart in his wicked eyes many a time. The very devil is in them. They are lasciviousness itself.

ABIGAIL ADAMS ON ALEXANDER HAMILTON

A vanity without bounds, and a jealousy capable of discoloring every object.

ALEXANDER HAMILTON ON JOHN ADAMS

JOHN ADAMS AND ALEXANDER HAMILTON HAD MUCH IN common. Both feuded with Thomas Jefferson. Both made crucial contributions to the Revolution—Adams in Congress and as a diplomat in Europe, Hamilton in the army as a top aide to George Washington. Both had grave doubts about unchecked democracy, and Jeffersonians would accuse both of being secret monarchists. One might conclude that Adams and Hamilton were, if not friends, at least allies.

Yet Adams and Hamilton detested each other far more than either disliked Jefferson.

AS THE FIRST PRESIDENTIAL ELECTION APPROACHED, WITH George Washington the inevitable choice as president and Adams the likely vice president, Hamilton wrote that Adams's election was unlikely to "disturb the harmony of the administration." This was in part because the vice president would have virtually no role in Washington's administration; Adams would complain that his was "the most insignificant office that ever the invention of man contrived or his imagination conceived." Hamilton, meanwhile, became secretary of the treasury and the president's most trusted adviser. Even after Hamilton returned to his private law practice in 1794, he remained the unofficial leader of the Federalist Party and continued to influence administration policy through his relationships with cabinet members and the president.

When Washington announced his retirement, both Adams and Hamilton wanted to succeed him. Hamilton knew he couldn't win: he had a well-deserved reputation as too divisive. And Adams, much as he disparaged the vice presidency, knew it had one major perk: he was, as he told his wife Abigail, "heir apparent."

In 1796, the Federalists chose Adams and Thomas Pinckney, the former governor of South Carolina, to face Republicans Jefferson and Aaron Burr. Both parties understood that this was a contest between Adams and Jefferson, but the Constitution made no distinction between votes for president and for vice president.

Hamilton jumped at the loophole. Anticipating he would be better able to control Pinckney, whom he described as having "a temper far more discreet and conciliatory than that of Mr. Adams," Hamilton quietly urged Federalist electors to withhold a few votes from Adams and make Pinckney president.

When the electoral votes were counted early in 1797, Adams became president with 71. Jefferson became vice president with 68. Pinckney, despite Hamilton's lobbying, finished with just 59 votes. Still, the Adamses, who had heard reports of Hamilton's efforts, were irate. "Beware of that spare Cassius," Abigail warned John, quoting Shakespeare and comparing Hamilton to the man who conspired against Caesar. "I have read his heart in his wicked eyes many a time. The very devil is in them. They are lasciviousness itself."

That summer, news broke of a scandal involving an affair Hamilton had had with a married woman, whose husband then blackmailed him. For the Adamses, this confirmed that Hamilton was lasciviousness itself. John Adams wanted nothing to do with him, and when Hamilton wrote him a long letter full of advice, the new president entirely ignored it.

However, Hamilton retained a great deal of indirect influence. Adams, hoping for a smooth transition, kept on members of Washington's cabinet, and these men—Secretary of State Timothy Pickering, Secretary of the Treasury Oliver Wolcott, and Secretary of War James McHenry—continued to defer to Hamilton.

The biggest policy differences between Hamilton and Adams

were over foreign affairs. Hamilton, like other "High Federalists," was appalled both by the French Revolution and by the support of Republicans like Jefferson for the French. He called for war preparations. Adams sought to avoid war and tried to steer a neutral path between the High Federalists and the Republicans as well as between England and France.

After a series of attacks on American ships prompted fears that the French might invade America, Hamilton called for creating an army of 50,000 men. Adams was highly skeptical. "At present," he wrote Secretary of War McHenry, "there is no more prospect of seeing a French army here than there is in heaven." Adams preferred building an American navy and thought Hamilton's proposal "one of the wildest extravagances of a knight errant." Congress followed Hamilton's lead and in May 1798 authorized an army, though of only 10,000 men.

The obvious choice to lead the army was Washington, and he agreed to accept the command. But it was generally understood that Washington, aged sixty-six and ailing, would not actually take command unless the French invaded. So Washington's chief deputy would in effect be in charge of the army, and Washington made clear that the man he wanted for the job was Hamilton.

"By some he is considered as an ambitious man, and therefore a dangerous one," Washington wrote Adams. "That he is ambitious I shall readily grant, but it is of that laudable kind which prompts a man to excel in whatever he takes in hand. He is enterprising, quick in his perceptions, and his judgment intuitively great: qualities essential to a great military character, and therefore...his loss will be irreparable."

Adams was furious. "If I should consent to the appointment of Hamilton as second in rank," he wrote Wolcott, "I should consider it...most difficult to justify." Adams went on, xenophobically, to tell Wolcott that Hamilton had not been born in the United States (true) and that "his rank in the late army was comparatively very low" (not true). Adams then added some old lines about John Calvin, which he clearly thought applied to Hamilton: "'Some think on Calvin heaven's own spirit fell, / While others deem him instrument of hell.'"

Adams never sent the letter to Wolcott; in the end, he saw no way to buck Washington, and he gave Hamilton the command. But there is no reason to doubt that, by this time in 1798, he indeed considered Hamilton an instrument of hell.

Adams was right to worry about Hamilton. Under Washington, first in the army and then in the cabinet, Hamilton operated within strict limits. But with Washington relinquishing any active role, Hamilton now, as his biographer Ron Chernow put it, "began to indulge in wild flights of fantasy and to resemble more the military adventurer of Republican mythology." When no French invasion materialized, Hamilton's ambitions turned to invading French and Spanish colonies in America.

When Adams failed to support any of these ventures or to raise the additional troops Hamilton requested, Hamilton abandoned any pretense of deferring to the president. In June 1799, he urged the cabinet members to ignore the commander in chief and make plans on their own. "If the chief is too desultory," Hamilton wrote McHenry, "his ministers ought to be the more united and steady and well settled in some reasonable system of measures." Besides, Hamilton continued, "we ought certainly to look to the possession of the Floridas and Louisiana—and we ought to squint at South America."

"That man," Abigail Adams wrote, "would in my mind become a second Bonaparte if he was possessed of equal power."

In 1799, Adams pulled the rug out from under Hamilton and his army. Against the advice of his cabinet, the president announced he intended to send a peace mission to France.

Stunned, Hamilton confronted Adams in person. They met in a Trenton, New Jersey boardinghouse, since the federal government had fled from Philadelphia because of an outbreak of yellow fever. Adams's account of the October meeting probably exaggerated how calm the president was but was undoubtedly accurate in portraying how upset Hamilton was. Hamilton spoke "with such agitation and violent action," Adams recalled, "that I really pitied him, instead of being displeased… I treated him throughout with great mildness and civility; but after he took leave, I could not help reflecting in my own mind on the total ignorance he had betrayed of everything in Europe, in France, England, and elsewhere."

Hamilton next appealed to Washington, in retirement but widely revered. But the ex-president had by this time concluded there that would be no war with France and that there was no need for Hamilton's army. In early May 1800, Adams began firing the Hamiltonians in his cabinet. McHenry recorded his confrontation with Adams, quoting the president as calling Hamilton "the greatest intriguant in the world—a man devoid of every moral principle—a bastard, and as much a foreigner as Gallatin." (Gallatin, a Republican from Pennsylvania, was born in Switzerland.) Continued Adams: "You are subservient to Hamilton, who ruled Washington, and would still rule if he could. Washington saddled me with three secretaries who would control me, but I shall take care of that."

That same month, Adams began disbanding Hamilton's army.

In September, Adams's peace mission paid off: the French agreed to stop attacking American ships. The mission, Adams declared, was "the most splendid diamond in my crown; or, if anyone thinks this expression too monarchical, I will say the most brilliant feather in my cap."

But Hamilton would soon have his revenge.

———◆◆◆◆◆———

THE ELECTION OF 1800 PITTED ADAMS AGAINST JEFFERSON. THIS time, Hamilton made no secret of his preference for anyone other than Adams. His first choice was another Pinckney from South Carolina, Charles Cotesworth Pinckney, but even a Republican—even Jefferson—would be better than Adams.

"If we must have an enemy at the head of the government, let it be one whom we can oppose and for whom we are not responsible, who will not involve our party in the disgrace of his foolish and bad measures," Hamilton wrote to Theodore Sedgwick, a Massachusetts Federalist. This was in May 1800.

Three months later, Hamilton wrote directly to Adams. "It has been repeatedly mentioned to me that you have, on different occasions, asserted the existence of a British faction in this country… and that you have sometimes named me, at other times plainly alluded to me, as one of this description of persons." Then, in language that could easily be interpreted as leading up to challenging the president of the United States to a duel, Hamilton demanded that Adams deny having made the accusation or provide proof.

Wisely, Adams did not respond.

In October 1800, Hamilton's vendetta against Adams went public, in the form of a "Letter from Alexander Hamilton, Concerning the Public Conduct and Character of John Adams, Esq., President of the United States." Possibly, Hamilton originally intended to circulate the letter selectively to influential Federalists, but once some of it leaked to Republican editors, he decided to publish it in its entirety as a fifty-four-page pamphlet.

The letter was, as Chernow put it, "an extended tantrum in print." Adams, Hamilton wrote, had "an imagination sublimated and eccentric; propitious neither to the regular display of sound judgment, nor to steady perseverance in a systematic plan of conduct."

Hamilton lambasted Adams for his handling of foreign

affairs and his treatment of his cabinet, but again and again he returned to his emotional imbalance—"the disgusting egotism, the distempered jealousy, and the ungovernable indiscretion of Mr. Adams's temper."

Hamilton concluded his letter, confusingly, by urging Federalist electors to cast votes for both Pinckney and Adams. Still, the letter revealed the gaping divide in the Federalist Party. Republicans were elated and thought the letter would ensure their victory. Adams, too, believed it had cost him the election. Many historians doubt it had, since many state legislatures had already chosen their presidential electors before the letter was published. More fundamentally, the Republican victory—Jefferson's "revolution of 1800"—was the result of the broad trend toward the increasing democratization of American politics and away from the elitism of the Federalists.

There's no doubt, however, that the letter hastened the decline of the Federalist Party and of Hamilton's already waning influence. His efforts to destroy Adams's political career ended up destroying his own.

As for Adams, though he did not respond immediately to the letter, he was no more capable than Hamilton of repressing his rage indefinitely. In 1806, two years after Hamilton's death, Adams wrote Dr. Benjamin Rush:

Although I...suffered to pass without animadversion in silent contempt the base insinuations of vanity and a hundred lies besides published in a pamphlet against me by an insolent cox-comb who rarely dined in good company, where there was good wine, without getting silly and vaporing about his adminis-tration like a young girl about her brilliants and trinkets, yet I lose all patience when I think of a bastard brat of a Scotch peddler... This creature was in a delirium of ambition...had fixed his eyes on the highest station in America, and he hated every man, young or old, who stood in his way.

THOMAS PAINE

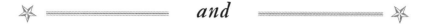 *and*

GEORGE WASHINGTON

And as to you, sir, treacherous in private friendship (for so you have been to me...) and a hypocrite in public life, the world will be puzzled to decide whether you are an apostate or an impostor? Whether you have abandoned good principles, or whether you ever had any?

THOMAS PAINE TO GEORGE WASHINGTON

NEAR THE END OF WASHINGTON'S SECOND TERM, THOMAS Jefferson complained to James Madison that the president "is fortunate to get off just as the bubble is bursting, leaving others to hold the bag," and that Washington "will have his usual good fortune of reaping credit from the good acts of others, and leaving to them that of his errors."

But Jefferson's mutterings to Madison were strictly private. Washington was, as historian Joseph Ellis put it, "the Foundingest Father of them all," and amid all their feuds, no leading founder dared attack Washington publicly. Except Thomas Paine.

IN EARLY JANUARY 1776, WITH THE CONTINENTAL CONGRESS unable to make up its mind about independence, Washington was short of money, troops, arms, and ammunition. "I have often thought how much happier I should have been," he complained, "if, instead of accepting a command under such circumstances, I had taken my musket upon my shoulder and entered the ranks, or…had retired to the backcountry and lived in a wigwam."

Washington's mood—and that of his countrymen—was brightened by the publication of Paine's short pamphlet, *Common Sense.* Paine's pamphlet recast the Revolution as about more than British policies or taxes, or even about Great Britain and America. What America was fighting for was freedom.

"We have it in our power to begin the world over again," Paine proclaimed. "The birthday of a new world is at hand."

By July, hundreds of thousands had read *Common Sense*—proportionally equivalent to more than twenty million today. Congress declared independence, and Americans flocked to the cause. Paine's work, Washington wrote, "is working a powerful change…in the minds of many men."

Paine's pen, his contemporaries and historians generally agree, was as important to the Revolution as Washington's sword.

Paine became a brigadier in Washington's army. And just as Washington refused pay for his position as commander in chief, Paine donated his *Common Sense* profits to the Continental Army.

As 1776 drew to a close, Washington again needed Paine's help. Having retreated through New Jersey, the army (including Paine) was holed up on the Pennsylvania side of the Delaware River. By the light of a campfire, Paine wrote *The American Crisis*.

"These are the times that try men's souls," he wrote in the first of the thirteen essays. "The summer soldier and the sunshine patriot will, in this crisis, shrink from the service of his country; but he that stands it now deserves the love and thanks of man and woman. Tyranny, like hell, is not easily conquered; yet we have this consolation with us, that the harder the conflict, the more glorious the triumph."

The pamphlet appeared in December and slowed the flow of militiamen who were giving up and heading home. On Christmas Eve, Washington ordered the essay read aloud to the troops. With Paine's words echoing in their minds, the troops crossed the icy Delaware River, surprised the Hessian mercenaries in Trenton, and won a decisive victory.

A year later, as Washington and his troops suffered through the winter at Valley Forge, some officers and members of the Continental Congress maneuvered to replace the commander in chief. Paine again rallied support for the general, praising his "unabated fortitude" in the fifth of the *American Crisis* essays.

Washington, in turn, came to Paine's aid when, after the war, Paine desperately needed money. Unlike Washington, who had inherited money and married the richest woman in Virginia, and could therefore easily afford to serve without pay, Paine had arrived in America as a working-class immigrant. When the war ended, he was broke. Washington lobbied Congress and the states on Paine's behalf.

"That his *Common Sense* and many of his [*American Crisis* essays] were well timed and had a happy effect upon the public mind, none…will deny," he wrote. "Does not common justice then point to some compensation?"

Congress granted Paine $3,000 and New York gave him some property, but neither was enough to keep Paine in America. The next frontier for the new world he envisioned was the Old World, and Paine was determined to be a part of the revolution in Europe. He returned to England, where he wrote the first part of *The Rights of Man*, defending the French Revolution and calling for a revolution in England. *Rights of Man* was published in London on February 22, 1791—Washington's birthday—and dedicated to the president.

<hr />

FOR REPUBLICANS LIKE JEFFERSON, THE FRENCH REVOLUTION WAS an extension of the American, and *Rights of Man* was an extension of *Common Sense*. Jefferson was "extremely pleased to find…that something is at length to be publicly said against the political heresies which have sprung up among us." When Jefferson's comments appeared in the American edition of *Rights of Man*, Federalists were outraged. Already stung by Republican claims that they were anti-French, pro-British, would-be monarchists, leading Federalists assumed (correctly) that Jefferson's criticisms were aimed at them.

As usual, Washington tried to remain above the fray, but, like other Federalists, he worried about the French Revolution "running into extremes." The president began distancing himself from Paine. He did not acknowledge Paine's dedication of *Rights of Man* until May 1792. Even then, Washington explained to Paine that he had been too busy to read the work. "Let it suffice, therefore," he wrote, "to say that I rejoice in the information of your personal prosperity."

Washington's fears of the French Revolution running into extremes were soon borne out. Even Paine was too moderate for the increasingly radical French revolutionaries. Though he was surely no monarchist, Paine argued that Louis XVI ought not to be executed. On Christmas Eve of 1793, in the midst of what came to be known as the Reign of Terror, Paine was arrested in Paris.

Confined to an eight-by-ten cell, Pained watched his fellow inmates sent to their deaths. "I should be tempted to curse the day I knew America," he despaired to James Monroe, America's ambassador to France. "By contributing to her liberty I have lost my own, and yet her government beholds my situation in silence."

After ten months, Paine was freed. Weakened by typhus and other illnesses he had contracted in prison, he moved in with the Monroes, still bitter about what he perceived as America's indifference to his ordeal. He felt especially betrayed by Washington.

In July 1796, not long after Monroe had suggested it was

time for Paine to move out, the ambassador wrote to James Madison. Paine, Monroe worried, was increasingly convinced that Washington had "winked at his imprisonment and even wished he might die in jail," perhaps in an effort to steer a neutral course between England and France.

Monroe was right to worry. Paine wrote an angry letter to Washington, blaming him for turning his back on him.

Paine was not the only one to turn on Washington. Republicans vehemently objected to the Jay Treaty of 1794. The treaty settled a number of disputes between the United States and England over boundaries and debts and British interference with American trade, but Republicans thought the treaty made too many concessions to Great Britain and undercut American neutrality. Republican newspapers such as Benjamin Franklin Bache's *Aurora* did not hesitate to blame Washington, and Jefferson privately complained about Washington to Madison.

Paine's fury would not be constrained in private correspondence. When Washington didn't answer his letter, Paine sent it to Bache, who printed an excerpt in the *Aurora* in October 1796 and the entire letter as a pamphlet in February 1797.

Paine's letter portrayed Washington's failure to come to his aid as part of a larger defect. "The character which Mr. Washington has attempted to act in the world is a sort of non-describable chameleon-colored thing called prudence," Paine wrote. "It is, in many cases, a substitute for principle, and is so nearly allied to hypocrisy that it easily slides into it."

Washington was "treacherous in private friendship (for so you have been to me, and that in the day of danger) and a hypocrite in public life." The world would be "puzzled to decide whether you are an apostate or an impostor? Whether you have abandoned good principles or whether you ever had any."

At times Paine stopped addressing Washington and made clear he was out to show the world the reality behind the heroic image: "It has some time been known by those who know him that he has no friendships, that he is incapable of forming any; he can serve or desert a man, or a cause, with constitutional indifference; and it is this cold hermaphrodite faculty that imposed itself upon the world, and was credited a while by enemies, as by friends, for prudence, moderation, and impartiality."

Paine attacked not only Washington's character but also his military record: "Had it not been for the aid received from France… your cold and unmilitary conduct…would in all probability have lost America… You slept away your time in the field till the finances of the country were completely exhausted, and you have but little share in the glory of the final event."

Whether Washington actually "winked" at Paine's imprisonment is not known. He never answered Paine's letter or even acknowledged receiving it, though he described the printed version as "absolute falsehoods."

As to Paine's broader attack on Washington's character, there is no doubt that Washington valued prudence, even aloofness—and this certainly added to his iconic stature. "He is in our textbooks and our wallets, but not our hearts," wrote Richard Brookhiser, one of his biographers.

———◆✦◈✦◆———

PAINE'S LETTER DID MORE DAMAGE TO HIS OWN REPUTATION THAN to Washington's. Federalist newspapers blasted the letter as what "you might expect from a traitorous scribbler, saturated with brandy."

When Jefferson became president in 1801, he offered to have a United States warship take Paine across the Atlantic, and that led to more anti-Paine and anti-Jefferson diatribes. Paine finally returned to America in 1802.

By then, Washington was dead and his apotheosis complete. Crowds filled memorial services throughout the country in 1799 and 1800. Washington was, as Henry Lee's famous eulogy put it, "first in war—first in peace—and first in the hearts of his countrymen."

In contrast, when Paine died in 1809, six mourners attended his funeral. Indeed, he lived his last years in relative obscurity. Partly this was because, unlike better remembered founders, Paine was relatively poor. Partly it was because he was primarily a writer and not a political leader. And partly it was because his writings antagonized not only Federalists, who never forgave his attack on Washington, but also Republicans, who were uncomfortable with some of his more radical ideas, especially his condemnation of organized religion and his support for a broad-based democracy.

Even Jefferson found Paine too radical. When asked for permission to print their correspondence, Jefferson refused. "Not for the world," he exclaimed. "Into what a nest of hornets would it thrust my head!"

"In the comic-book version of history," wrote historian Jill Lepore, "Paine is Aquaman to Washington's Superman and Jefferson's Batman; we never find out how he got his superpowers, and he only shows up when they need someone who can swim." But, Lepore added, "Paine's contributions to the nation's founding would be hard to overstate."

ROGER GRISWOLD

and

MATTHEW LYON

I called him a scoundrel and struck him with my cane, and pursued him with more than twenty blows on his head and back until he got possession of a pair of tongs...

ROGER GRISWOLD DESCRIBING HIS FIGHT
WITH FELLOW CONGRESSMAN MATTHEW LYON

THE BITTER DIVISIONS THAT AROSE DURING THE YEARS OF John Adams's presidency extended well beyond the Adams-Hamilton-Jefferson triangle. With George Washington retired and no longer around to unite the competing factions, factions turned into Federalists and Republicans, and the parties sometimes seemed at the verge of disuniting the United States. Early in 1798, the tensions turned violent, when Roger Griswold attacked Matthew Lyon right inside the halls of Congress.

THE FIRST INCIDENT TOOK PLACE ON JANUARY 30. ACCORDING TO a congressional committee appointed to investigate, Lyon, the Republican congressman from Vermont, was talking to the Speaker of the House during a recess. "He spoke loud enough to be heard by all those who were near him," the committee reported, "as if he intended to be heard by them."

What Lyon loudly said was that the representatives of the state of Connecticut "acted in opposition to the interests and opinion of nine-tenths of their constituents; that they were pursuing their own private views, without regarding the interests of the people… that the people of that state were blinded or deceived by those representatives…being lulled asleep by the opiates which the members from that state administered to them." Lyon added various other "expressions equally tending to derogate from the political integrity of the representatives of Connecticut."

Lyon, who was a newspaper publisher as well as a congressman, added that "if he should go into Connecticut, and manage a press there six months, although the people of that state were not fond of revolutionary principles, he could effect a revolution, and turn out the present representatives."

Among those Lyon hoped would overhear his remarks was Roger Griswold, a Federalist congressman from Connecticut. Lyon intended to provoke Griswold—and in that he succeeded.

Griswold responded: "If you go into Connecticut, you had better wear your wooden sword." Griswold was alluding to a story that Lyon, while a soldier during the Revolution, had been court-martialed for cowardice and sentenced to carry a wooden sword.

Lyon was especially sensitive about the wooden sword, because the story had been circulating in Federalist newspapers before Griswold used it to insult him, and it was certainly not a full or fair account of Lyon's service in the war.

Lyon had served, courageously, under Ethan Allen and Benedict Arnold when they captured Fort Ticonderoga in May 1775. In July 1776, he was ordered to protect a storehouse near the Canadian border. With hostile Indians nearby, the men under Lyon's command mutinied, and as Lyon told the congressional committee, "I did not think it my duty to resist alone."

This led to Lyon's discharge from the army. But there may never have been a wooden sword, and at least some of Lyon's superiors did not believe his court-martial was fair, as evidenced by Lyon's subsequent appointment as paymaster to a Continental regiment.

In any case, Lyon did not directly respond to Griswold's comment about the sword. Instead, he continued to talk to the Speaker, pointedly noting that he had lived in Connecticut before moving to Vermont, and that he had never failed to convince the people of Connecticut of the merits of his arguments. Griswold interrupted again, asking "if he fought them with his wooden sword." At this point, "Mr. Lyon spat in his face."

After the committee delivered its report, Congress spent the next couple of weeks debating whether to expel Lyon. Congressman Christopher Champlin, a Federalist from Rhode

Island, said that Lyon's behavior "tended to degrade the members of that House from the rank of men, and to reduce them to a level with the meanest reptile that crawled upon the earth." Congressman Samuel Dana, a Federalist from Connecticut, urged his colleagues to deal with Lyon "as citizens removed impurities and filth from their docks and wharves."

Congressman Albert Gallatin, a Republican from Pennsylvania, conceded that Lyon might "be disqualified for polite society" but argued this was not sufficient reason to deprive his constituents of his vote. In general, Republicans suspected Federalists were using the issue to try to get rid of a Republican vote.

On February 12, the House voted 52 to 44 to expel Lyon. Since the Constitution required a two-thirds vote to expel, the motion failed.

Griswold then decided to take matters into his own hands. Here's how he later described the events of February 15:

As soon as I saw [Lyon] in his seat, I took my cane and walked across the floor in front of the speaker's chair... He saw me before I struck him, and was endeavoring to draw a sword cane when I gave him the first blow. I called him a scoundrel and struck him with my cane, and pursued him with more than twenty blows on his head and back until he got possession of a pair of tongs, when I threw him down and after giving him several blows with my fist, I was taken off by his friends.

Lyon was "very much bruised" and had "blood running down his face," Griswold added.

The spectacle of two Congressmen brawling, one with a cane and the other with fireplace tongs, was irresistible to cartoonists and satirists. One poem, titled "Lyon and Griswold: Battle of the Wooden Sword!!" included the following stanzas:

> Against his will, when Roger still
> Saw Matthew was not outed,
> And from his seat did not retreat,
> He swore he should be routed.
>
> So next he went, with bad intent,
> And entered Congress hall in,
> He took his cane, to crack the brain,
> And lay old Matthew sprawling.

The wooden sword was not the underlying source of hostility between Lyon and Griswold, or between Republicans and Federalists. Republicans had been ridiculing Federalists as aristocrats, as monarchists, and as Tories. In June 1797, months before the Griswold-Lyon incidents, Republicans had taken a stand against various forms of deference to the president. Lyon had been among those who most adamantly objected to presidential pomp.

He explained he had "spent a great part of his life amongst a people whose love of a plainness of manners forbids all pageantry."

Griswold fit the Republicans' image of an aristocrat, having gone to Yale and then studied law in his father's office. And Lyon fit the Federalists' image of a democrat, a term Republicans were starting to embrace but which still conjured up images of mob rule.

Lyon had left Ireland in 1764 and arrived in Connecticut as an indentured servant (he was the first former indentured servant to serve in Congress). He seized what opportunities he found, moving to Vermont, where land was cheap, and eventually building mills and foundries. But he remained very much a man whose "plainness of manners" might have made him comfortable in the later White House of Andrew Jackson but not in the President's House of John Adams.

Federalists were also disturbed by Lyon's position as publisher of a newspaper. Some of this was snobbery: a printer—an artisan— had no place in Congress. Some of it was fear: the opposition press was growing in influence and would eventually play a key role in the demise of the Federalist Party. It was probably no coincidence that Griswold brought up the wooden sword after hearing Lyon brag about how his press could sway the people of Connecticut.

To Federalists, men like Lyon had neither the education nor the breeding nor the virtue to govern. Lyon was, Griswold said, "a mere beast and the fool of the play." That Griswold considered Lyon inferior was clear from his choice of weapon. Had he considered

Lyon an equal, he might have challenged him to a duel; instead, he chose a cane.

The Federalists were not wrong to assume Lyon had entered politics at least in part to advance his own personal interests. He was most definitely not the disinterested ideal statesman that Federalists—or for that matter, aristocratic Southern Republicans like Jefferson or Madison—envisioned running the nation. In Vermont, Lyon used his position as clerk of the Court of Confiscation to get inside information on Loyalist property, which he then bought for himself. In the Vermont legislature, he tried to secure subsidies for iron manufacturing, and it was not a coincidence that he owned a factory. And his newspaper was above all a mouthpiece for Lyon's campaigns for office.

Still, the Federalist insults, which had been going on for months before the Lyon-Griswold fracas, revealed a definitely undemocratic and often nativist bias against a self-made immigrant. During a June 1797 debate, for example, after Lyon suggested deleting a clause from a resolution about John Adams's conduct toward foreign nations, Congressman John Allen of Connecticut responded that "there was American blood enough in the House to approve of this clause, and American accent enough to pronounce it."

America was becoming an increasingly democratic and diverse nation, whether Federalists liked it or not, and the future belonged to men like Lyon. "Conquest had led [my] country to independence," Lyon said in response to Allen's remarks, "and being independent, [I] called no man's blood in question."

LYON'S IMMEDIATE FUTURE WAS DARKENED BY THE SEDITION Act of July 14, 1798, which made it a crime to "write, print, utter or publish…any false, scandalous and malicious writing or writings against the government of the United States, or either house of the Congress of the United States, or the president of the United States, with intent to defame the said government, or either house…or the said president, or to bring them…into contempt or disrepute."

The Federalist-controlled Congress passed the act with the intent of silencing Republican newspapers like Lyon's. Lyon was the first person tried for violating the Act, after he published a piece in which he accused the president of "an unbounded thirst for ridiculous pomp, foolish adulation, and selfish avarice." He was convicted and sentenced to four months in jail and a fine of one thousand dollars.

This did not silence Lyon. From his jail cell, he ran a successful campaign for reelection through his new magazine, *The Scourge of Aristocracy*. More generally, the Sedition Act failed to slow the rise of Republican newspapers or the Republican Party. In 1800, Thomas Jefferson defeated John Adams in the presidential election. The quirk in the Electoral College system remained, leading to a tie between Jefferson and the Republican vice presidential candidate, Aaron Burr. This threw the election into the House of Representatives, where members voted by state, with Vermont being last on the roll call. The last vote cast in the House—the vote that made Jefferson president—was cast by Vermont's sole representative, Matthew Lyon.

Some Federalists, appalled by Jefferson's presidency and unwilling to accept their status as a minority party, at least nationally, plotted to secede. Among their leaders was Roger Griswold.

By 1804, Griswold was openly calling for "a union of the northern states." He warned that "democracy is making daily inroads upon us" and that "there can be no safety to the northern states without a separation from the confederacy." There were not enough embittered Federalists to bring about a northern confederacy, but Griswold continued to resist Jefferson and his successors. He opposed the War of 1812 and, as governor of Connecticut, refused to put his state's militia under the command of federal officers. He died later that year.

WILLIAM COBBETT

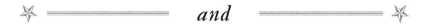 *and*

THOMAS PAINE

*He has done all the mischief he can in the world...
Whenever and wherever he breathes his last, he will
excite neither sorrow nor compassion; no friendly hand
will close his eyes, not a groan will be uttered, not a tear
will be shed.*

WILLIAM COBBETT ON THOMAS PAINE

MATTHEW LYON WAS THE FIRST PERSON TO BE TRIED UNDER the Sedition Act, but no writer was more feared by Federalists than Thomas Paine. And for sheer vitriol, no writer could match Paine's fearsome antagonist, William Cobbett.

Paine arrived from England in 1774 with little more than a letter of recommendation from Benjamin Franklin, whom he had met in London. Within just a few years, his *Common Sense* and *American Crisis* essays were widely credited with inspiring Americans to "begin the world over again."

Paine's later writings drove home what he had in mind for his new world. *The Rights of Man* defended the French Revolution and called for revolution in England. *The Age of Reason* took on organized religion.

This was far too radical for many Americans. Paine was, John Adams wrote, "begotten by a wild boar on a bitch wolf," adding that "never before in any age of the world" had there been "such a career of mischief."

As insults go, that might seem hard to top, but Cobbett certainly tried. Like Paine, Cobbett was a refugee from England and an extremely popular author.

"How Tom gets a living now, or what brothel he inhabits, I know not," Cobbett wrote in 1796, in *An Antidote for Tom Paine's Theological and Political Poison.* Continued Cobbett: "Whether his carcass is at last to be suffered to rot on the earth, or to be dried in the air, is of very little consequence… Like *Judas* he will be remembered by posterity; men will learn to express all that is base, malignant, treacherous, unnatural and blasphemous, by the single monosyllable, *Paine.*"

❖

Paine returned to England in 1787 to work for revolution there. *Rights of Man* led to a warrant for his arrest on charges of treason, and in 1792 he fled to France, where he had already been elected to the National Assembly. Wrote Cobbett: "Thomas's having merited death, or, at least, transportation in England, was a strong recommendation to him in France, whose newly enlightened inhabitants seem to have conceived a wonderful partiality for all that's vile."

For once, Paine was not radical enough. After he argued that Louis XVI ought not to be executed, Paine was jailed in Paris. Feeling abandoned by his fellow founders, Paine wrote his bitter denunciation of Washington, which he sent to his American publisher Benjamin Franklin Bache. Bache had inherited his printing equipment and his name from his grandfather, Benjamin Franklin. Bache also inherited Franklin's affection for Paine, printing *Rights of Man* and, in October 1796, Paine's letter to Washington. Bache's publication of Paine's letter was part of a growing press war between Federalist and Republican newspapers. For these newspapers, there was no pretense of objectivity; editors were openly and actively partisan.

The main Federalist newspapers were John Fenno's *Gazette of the United States* and Cobbett's *Porcupine's Gazette*. Thomas Jefferson was fully aware of their influence. "It is hardly necessary to caution you to let nothing of mine get before the public," he wrote John Taylor in 1798. "A single sentence got hold of by the Porcupines will suffice to abuse and persecute me in their papers for months."

Republicans countered with Philip Freneau's *National Gazette* and Bache's Philadelphia *General Advertiser* (later renamed the *Aurora General Advertiser*).

The newspaper wars occasionally led to actual violence. In the spring of 1797, Federalist Clement Humphries assaulted Bache on the Philadelphia waterfront. Ultimately, the Federalists moved the battlefront to Congress, passing the Sedition Act of 1798, which outlawed "any false, scandalous and malicious writing or writings against the government." The Federalists used the act to prosecute not only Lyon but also Bache. After Bache died from yellow fever in 1798, they went after his successor, William Duane, who was indicted under the Sedition Act as well as beaten by a gang of Federalist supporters.

In the long run, the Sedition Act did not stop the growth of the Republican press, nor the Republican Party. But neither Bache nor Paine recovered from the newspaper wars of the 1790s. Their criticism of Washington went too far for most Americans, as did Paine's attack on organized religion. Before his death, Bache had lost most of the goodwill he had inherited from his grandfather. Paine returned to America in 1802 but found himself isolated from his fellow founders.

———————————

COBBETT WAS AN UNLIKELY ADVERSARY FOR PAINE. THEIR BACKgrounds were similar; though born twenty-six years after Paine, Cobbett, too, came from a working class background and was appalled by social injustice. His first work was an exposé of corruption in the British military. After it was published, Cobbett had to flee England for France and then America. He arrived in America very much a follower of Paine.

It was in America that Cobbett veered off Paine's path. "Instead of that perfect freedom, and that amiable simplicity, of which Paine had given me so flattering a description, I found myself placed under a set of petty, mean despots, ruling by the powers given them by a perversion of the law of England."

Paine saw the imperfections of the world and concluded that what was needed was revolution. Cobbett saw the same imperfections and concluded that America was more corrupt than England and the English system of government was the best in the world. He defended his homeland with a passion that surpassed that of any Federalist of the 1790s and matched that of any loyalist during the Revolution. Democracy, he wrote under the byline of Peter Porcupine, was "absolutely worse than street sweepings, or the filth of common sewers." Cobbett went so far as to hang in the window of his print shop portraits of King George III and his ministers.

Cobbett's aggressive style, like Paine's, gained him a wide following. And Paine was his favorite target. "The most dangerous arguments of the infamous Paine," he wrote in 1799, "and the other seducers of the people, were built on their impudent misstatements respecting America."

Cobbett's attacks were both political and personal. Paine was an "infidel anarchist" and "a brutal and savage husband, and an unnatural father." Paine embraced the French Revolution for the same reason a criminal embraced chaos: "He had enjoyed partial revolts before, had seen doors and windows broken in, and had probably partaken of the pillage of some aristocratic stores and dwelling-houses; but to live in a continual state of insurrection…to sit seven days in the week issuing decrees for plunder, proscription, and massacre, was a luxurious life indeed!"

Paine, in France, did not respond to Cobbett's attacks. But Paine was aware of Peter Porcupine—or, as he referred to him, "Peter Skunk."

———◆➤◆◄◆———

AFTER LOSING A LIBEL SUIT, COBBETT FLED BACK TO LONDON. There he again discovered that the reality, this time of the English government, did not match the idealized version of it he had been writing about. He was again appalled by corruption and inequality, and when he wrote about it—in particular, about the army's use of flogging—he was found guilty of sedition and sentenced to prison. Now he decided that Paine had been right about everything all along.

Cobbett later wrote that it was Paine's 1796 essay on the English finance system that brought him back into Paine's fold. More likely, that essay was part of a more gradual process. Cobbett was disillusioned by much he saw in England and, like Paine, he was surely embittered by his time in prison.

"Paine observed very truly," Cobbett wrote in 1815, "that a rich government made a poor people." Cobbett committed himself to publish all of Paine's work, and he began research on a biography, never finished.

Cobbett was distraught at the thought that Paine would be forgotten, and he was right to worry. Even Jefferson had distanced himself from Paine. When Paine died in 1809, his death went largely unnoticed.

"Paine lies in a little hole under the grass and weeds of an obscure farm in America," bemoaned Cobbett. "There, however, he shall not lie, unnoticed, much longer... Never will England be what it ought to be, until the marble of [former prime minister William] Pitt's monument is converted into a monument to the memory of Paine."

And so it was that early one morning before sunrise in September 1819, Cobbett, his oldest son J. P., and a hired hand stumbled through the dark near the town of New Rochelle, outside New York City. They dug up Paine's corpse and, with the local authorities on their tail, sailed to England. At a customs inspection in Liverpool, Cobbett opened his luggage and announced: "There, gentlemen, are the mortal remains of the immortal Thomas Paine."

The British government did not embrace Cobbett's proposal for a monument to Paine. The press mocked Cobbett as ruthlessly as Cobbett had mocked others. Wrote the poet Lord Byron:

> In digging up your bones, Tom Paine,
> Will. Cobbett has done well:
> You visit him on earth again,
> He'll visit you in hell.

When Cobbett died in 1835, J. P. inherited the bones. Historians since have speculated about the fate of the remains, notably Paul Collins in his 2005 book about Paine's afterlife. They appear to have been scattered—like Paine's ideas—around the world.

AARON BURR

✳ ═══════════ *and* ═══════════ ✳

ALEXANDER HAMILTON

His private character is not defended by his most partial friends. He is bankrupt beyond redemption except by the plunder of his country. His public principles have no other spring or aim than his own aggrandizement.

ALEXANDER HAMILTON ON AARON BURR

THE RHETORIC OF MEN LIKE THOMAS PAINE AND WILLIAM COBBETT was so vituperative, the questions they raised so fundamental, that it is not surprising feuds would escalate to violence. Certainly this was the pattern the founders witnessed in France, where revolution begat terror. Perhaps, given the history of revolutions—and not just in France—what should surprise us is how rarely the politics of the early republic turned bloody.

But blood there was. Most notoriously, on the morning of July 11, 1804, Aaron Burr and Alexander Hamilton rowed across the Hudson River to an isolated spot in Weehawken, New Jersey. At the time, Burr was the vice president of the United States.

Hamilton's influence had waned, partly as a result of his self-destructive feud with John Adams, but the former treasury secretary was still deservedly renowned for his crucial roles in getting the Constitution ratified and in setting the economic course of the new nation.

Following the *code duello*, they stood ten paces apart and exchanged shots. Burr's bullet struck Hamilton on the side. "I am a dead man," Hamilton cried. He died the next day.

———◆◆◇◆◆———

They had not always been enemies. In 1776, when British forces landed in Manhattan, Captain Hamilton and his troops were trapped behind enemy lines. Lieutenant Colonel Burr, a native New Yorker who knew roads that the British did not, led Hamilton to safety. Burr may thus have saved Hamilton's life, or at least saved him from spending the war years as a prisoner.

Hamilton's first anti-Burr comments dated to 1789. Burr and Hamilton both supported Robert Yates during that year's campaign for New York governor, but when George Clinton defeated Yates, Burr accepted Clinton's offer to become attorney general. Hamilton concluded Burr was an unprincipled opportunist.

The relationship deteriorated further in 1791, when Burr defeated Hamilton's father-in-law to become a senator from New York. The next year was worse: Burr toyed with running for governor himself but then backed Clinton, again against Hamilton's preferred candidate. Later in 1792 Burr considered running for vice president. Hamilton was appalled.

"He is for or against nothing, but as it suits his interest or ambition," Hamilton wrote. "I feel it a religious duty to oppose his career." A few days later, Hamilton described Burr as an "embryo-Caesar."

Hamilton's suspicions that Burr could not be trusted were fueled by Burr's work to secure a state charter for the Manhattan Company. This appeared to be very much in the public interest. An epidemic of yellow fever had killed almost two thousand New Yorkers in 1798, and Burr was ostensibly backing the company so that it could provide purer water to city residents, thus preventing the spread of the disease. Burr enlisted the support both of his fellow Republicans and of Federalists, including Hamilton. Then, after many legislators had left for home, Burr added to the bill language allowing the company to use surplus capital for other purposes. In essence, he chartered a bank, and one which would compete with the federal bank that Hamilton had created.

Still, the hostility between Burr and Hamilton wasn't constant. In 1797, Burr may even have saved Hamilton's life a second time, this time by heading off a duel between Hamilton and James Monroe. Monroe was one of three congressmen who had investigated allegations that Hamilton had passed on privileged information and money to a shady character named James Reynolds, allowing Reynolds to make investments on Hamilton's behalf. Hamilton admitted to the congressmen that he had paid Reynolds but said it was blackmail: Reynolds, Hamilton explained, had demanded the money in return for keeping quiet about an affair Hamilton had with Reynolds's wife. When the scandal became public, Hamilton accused Monroe of leaking documents to the press. Monroe denied doing so, and their exchanges were increasingly threatening.

Burr calmed the waters. "If you…really believe," he wrote Monroe, "as I do, and think you must, that H. is innocent of the charge of any concern in speculation with Reynolds, it is my opinion that it will be an act of magnanimity and justice to say so." Monroe agreed and backed away from a duel.

In 1800, Burr and Hamilton were allies again. The two, both of whom were lawyers, represented Levi Weeks, a young man charged with murdering his fiancée. Hamilton and Burr argued the evidence against Weeks was circumstantial, and a jury found him not guilty.

HAMILTON'S ANTIPATHY TOWARD BURR RESURFACED IN THE wake of the 1800 presidential election. Thomas Jefferson had selected Burr as his running mate, calculating—correctly, it turned out—that Burr would deliver New York's electoral votes to the Republican ticket. The problem was that Jefferson and Burr tied with 73 votes each. This left the decision up to the House of Representatives, which was still controlled by Federalists.

Hamilton, of course, hated Jefferson. Within Washington's cabinet, the two had feuded constantly. Jefferson had opposed Hamilton's efforts to establish a national bank, and more fundamentally, to set what Hamilton saw as a stable course for the federal government. Hamilton feared that under Jefferson the American Revolution would follow the course of the French Revolution, and America would descend into anarchy.

Some Federalists wondered openly whether they might be better off with Burr than Jefferson. Burr was not as clearly wed to the Republican ideology as Jefferson; he would be more open to compromise. And Burr was from New York, not Virginia.

Hamilton disagreed, vigorously and repeatedly. As Hamilton saw it, Jefferson's principles may have been dangerous, but Burr had no principles at all.

"There is no doubt but that upon every virtuous and prudent calculation Jefferson is to be preferred," he wrote in December 1800. "He is by far not so dangerous a man and he has pretensions to character."

Hamilton continued:

> *As to Burr there is nothing in his favor. His private character is not defended by his most partial friends. He is bankrupt beyond redemption except by the plunder of his country. His public principles have no other spring or aim than his own aggrandizement... If he can, he will certainly disturb our institutions to secure to himself permanent power and with it wealth. He is truly the Cataline of America.*

The reference to Cataline would have been clear to members

of the founding generation, versed as they were in the classics. Cataline's crimes included incest, murdering family members, and conspiring to bring down the Roman republic.

Hamilton was equally harsh a month later:

Nothing has given me so much chagrin as the intelligence that the Federal [P]arty were thinking seriously of supporting Mr. Burr for president. I should consider the execution of the plan as...signing their own death warrant. Mr. Burr will probably make stipulations, but he will laugh in his sleeve while he makes them and he will break them the first moment it may serve his purpose...stable power and great wealth being his objects, and these being unattainable by means that the sober part of the Federalists will countenance, he will certainly deceive and disappoint them.

Concluded Hamilton: "He is certainly one of the most unprincipled men in the United States."

It took six rounds of voting for the House to choose a president. Finally, a Delaware Federalist withdrew his support for Burr, and Jefferson was elected.

How hard Burr and Hamilton tried to influence the House of Representatives remains a subject of debate among historians. Burr didn't actively try to reach a deal with Federalists, but neither did he put a stop to Federalist discussions about the possibility of a Burr presidency. Hamilton was certainly active in trying to kill any deal that would have made Burr president, but Hamilton's influence, even among Federalists, was no longer as great as when he had been Washington's most trusted cabinet member.

About this, though, there is no question: Burr knew what Hamilton was up to, and he would not forget it.

Hamilton did it again four years later.

After the 1800 election, Jefferson no longer trusted Burr, and well before the 1804 presidential election it was clear that he intended to replace Burr on the ticket. Burr decided to return to his political base and run for governor of New York. He again looked for support from both Republicans and Federalists. The latter included some New England Federalists who, like Connecticut's Roger Griswold, were so distressed by Jefferson's presidency that they were planning to secede from the union and create a new confederacy of northern states. Burr never endorsed secession, but he sympathized with the Northerners' concerns.

Hamilton was dismayed by talk of secession and assumed the worst of Burr—that Burr would use the governorship of New York as a stepping stone to the presidency of a northern confederacy. "The ill opinion of Jefferson and jealousy of the ambition of Virginia… are leading to an opinion that a dismemberment of the Union is expedient," Hamilton said at an 1804 meeting of Federalists. "It would probably suit Mr. Burr's views to promote this result to be the chief of the northern portion—and placed at the head of the state of New York no man would be more likely to succeed."

Burr lost the race for governor. Again it was debatable how much Hamilton was to blame, but again it was not debatable that Hamilton tried to undermine Burr. Burr was especially incensed by a letter published in the April 24, 1804, issue of the *Albany Register*. The letter, from a Charles Cooper, quoted Hamilton as calling Burr "a dangerous man, and one who ought not to be trusted with the reins of government." Cooper added, "I could detail to you a still more despicable opinion which General Hamilton has expressed of Mr. Burr."

Burr demanded Hamilton explain Cooper's remarks, in particular the "still more despicable opinion." Hamilton responded that Burr's demand was too vague, arguing: "the phrase 'still more despicable' admits of infinite shades, from very light to very dark." Hamilton's evasion further antagonized Burr, and the exchanges escalated until the duel was inevitable.

What the "more despicable opinion" was remains unclear. Some have speculated Hamilton said Burr was sleeping with his daughter, Theodosia. Ultimately, the specific insult was irrelevant. Burr was driven to the duel not by this one comment but by more than a dozen years of insults. "It is too well known that General H. had long indulged himself in illiberal freedom with my character," he explained a week after the duel. "He had a peculiar talent of saying things improper and offensive in such a manner as could not well be taken hold of."

Hamilton would not offer any clear denial of Cooper's statement, because he did indeed consider Burr despicable, and he had been saying so for years. Days before he met Burr at Weehawken, Hamilton set forth the reasons he wanted to avoid the duel and, possibly, his death: dueling was against his principles and illegal; his wife and children needed him, as did his creditors; and he had "no ill-will to Colonel Burr." But, he explained, he could not deny "my animadversions on the political principles, character, and views of Colonel Burr have been extremely severe, and on different occasions I…have made very unfavorable criticisms…of the private conduct of this gentleman."

—◆•×◦•◆—

HAMILTON'S DEATH MADE HIM A MARTYR FOR FEDERALISTS AND led to an outcry against dueling. Many had already seen it as an aristocratic anachronism; after Weehawken, it was increasingly seen as a glorified form of murder.

Burr was indicted for dueling and murder, and further disgraced by reports—still disputed—that Hamilton had intentionally aimed to miss. The vice president fled west, where gunfighting was more common and Hamilton was a symbol of the hated eastern establishment of bankers and land speculators.

Burr continues to be remembered mostly as his enemies, Hamilton and Jefferson, saw him, and there was much truth in their portrait of an opportunist whose loyalties were primarily to his own ambitions. But he deserves at least some appreciation for having managed, in an age whose ideological divisions were even greater than our own, to find ways to appeal to partisans of both sides.

Today, when tolerance for opposing views is again hard to come by, it's worth remembering words Burr supposedly spoke as he neared death. According to a nineteenth-century biographer, James Parton, Burr spent his last days reading books, among them *The Life and Opinions of Tristram Shandy, Gentleman* by Lawrence Sterne. In the novel, a character is tormented by a fly buzzing around his nose during dinner. He catches the fly, then tosses it out the window, saying: "This world surely is wide enough to hold both thee and me." As Parton tells the story, Burr, after reading *Tristram Shandy*, said: "I should have known that the world was wide enough for Hamilton and me."

AARON BURR

and

THOMAS JEFFERSON

*No man's history proves better the value of honesty. With
that, what might he not have been!*

THOMAS JEFFERSON ON AARON BURR

KILLING ALEXANDER HAMILTON SEVERELY LIMITED AARON BURR'S
options. "In New York I am to be disenfranchised and in New
Jersey hanged," he complained. "Having substantial objections
to both, I…shall seek another country." That country was the
American West.

What Burr did there remains a matter of much dispute. Not to
Thomas Jefferson, though. In January 1807, the president informed
Congress that Burr was behind a conspiracy to create a new nation,
partly out of Mexico and partly out of the American West. His
former vice president, Jefferson told Congress, was a traitor, his
guilt "beyond question."

FOR JEFFERSON, THE PRESIDENTIAL ELECTION OF 1800 WAS sufficient evidence that Burr could not be trusted.

Jefferson and Burr were running mates on the Republican ticket that faced the incumbent John Adams and Adams's fellow Federalist, Charles Cotesworth Pinckney. The Republicans were confident they would carry Jefferson's Virginia and the rest of the South, but they needed to make some inroads into the North. Burr, who had been New York's attorney general and then senator, could balance the ticket.

The strategy worked. Burr helped the Republicans carry New York and win the election.

The men who wrote the Constitution, despite all their feuding, did not believe in a party system; they assumed voters would simply choose the best man. Not until the Twelfth Amendment was ratified in 1804 did ballots specify which candidates were running for president and which for vice president. Before then, each member of the Electoral College simply cast two votes for president. The candidate with the most votes became president, and the candidate with the second most became vice president.

So in 1800, though the Republicans had chosen Burr as their vice presidential candidate, he ended up with the same 73 votes as Jefferson. The Constitution provided that, in the event of a tie, the election would be decided by the House of Representatives.

In December, before the final votes were in but anticipating the possibility of a tie, Burr sent a reassuring (and public) letter to Samuel Smith, a Republican from Maryland: "It is highly improbable that I shall have an equal number of votes with Mr. Jefferson," he wrote, "but if such should be the result, every man who knows me ought to know that I should utterly disclaim all competition." Burr understood that most voters had intended Jefferson to be president; any other outcome, he told Smith, would be "counteracting the wishes and expectations of the U.S."

Less than two weeks later, having learned that he and Jefferson were indeed tied, Burr was less clear about his intentions. He had been asked, he explained (again to Smith), whether he would turn down the presidency if the House chose him over Jefferson. "The question was unnecessary, unreasonable and impertinent," Burr bristled, "and I have therefore made no reply."

This was the opening for which Federalists had hoped. The Federalists still controlled the House of Representatives, since the Republicans who had been elected alongside Jefferson had not yet taken office, and the Federalists therefore had it in their power to choose the next president. They began discussing among themselves the comparative merits—or rather, demerits—of Jefferson and Burr.

Theodore Sedgwick, a Massachusetts Federalist and the Speaker of the House, suggested to Alexander Hamilton that Burr's lack of principles was preferable to Jefferson's principles. Unlike Jefferson, Burr "holds to no pernicious theories," Sedgwick wrote. "His very selfishness prevents his entertaining any mischievous predilections." Plus, as a New Yorker, Burr understood the needs of merchants and manufacturers far better than a Virginia plantation owner.

Hamilton, despite his feud with Jefferson, disliked Burr even more. Other Federalists weighed other options, which included negotiating with both Jefferson and Burr, or blocking the election of either.

Republicans feared the worse. Some began thinking about an armed march on the capital, should Jefferson be denied the presidency. Jefferson suspected Burr was offering jobs to some members of the House in return for their votes. If the Federalists tried to "reverse what has been understood to have been the wishes of the people as to their president and vice president," Jefferson worried, "this opens upon us an abyss at which every sincere patriot must shudder."

In the end, Federalists backed away from Burr, and it was Jefferson, of course, who became president.

Did Burr actually conspire to grab the presidency? There's no evidence he actively solicited Federalist votes, and his second letter to Smith can be interpreted as just an expression of annoyance about his being asked whether he would accept the presidency. But Burr certainly didn't discourage Federalists from considering him as an option.

Whatever Burr did or didn't do, Jefferson thought the worst of him. "I never indeed thought him an honest, frank-dealing man," he later wrote, "but considered him as a crooked gun, or other perverted machine, whose aim or shot you could never be sure of."

Jefferson made sure Burr's allies had no role in his administration. For the 1804 election, Jefferson replaced Burr on the Republican ticket with George Clinton.

AFTER HIS 1804 DUEL WITH HAMILTON, BURR HEADED WEST. There he met with military figures, including Andrew Jackson and James Wilkinson, commander of the U.S. forces in the West.

By 1805, the city of Washington was abuzz with rumors about Burr, usually involving military expeditions against Spanish territories in Texas and Florida. Jefferson again assumed the worst: that Burr was planning "the severance of the union of these states by the Allegheny Mountains." His suspicions seemed confirmed in November 1806 when Wilkinson sent the president a copy of a letter the general allegedly had received from Burr. The letter sounded like a plot for a revolution in the West, with Burr setting himself up as emperor of a new nation and offering to make Wilkinson his second in command. Jefferson collected evidence of the conspiracy and in January 1807 forwarded it to Congress.

"Burr's enterprise is the most extraordinary since the days of Don Quixote," Jefferson wrote. "It is so extravagant that those who know his understanding would not believe it if the proofs admitted doubt. He has meant to place himself on the throne of Montezuma."

Burr was charged with treason and brought to Richmond. Jefferson was almost gleeful and more than a little sanctimonious: "No man's history proves better the value of honesty. With that, what might he not have been!"

Jefferson threw the weight of the presidency behind the

prosecution. He declared Burr guilty before the trial even began, and he advised prosecutors throughout the trial. The prosecution was nonetheless working at a disadvantage. For starters, the judge was Chief Justice John Marshall, a Jefferson foe. Marshall ruled that treason required an overt act and that Burr's plans—whatever they were—could not be brought into evidence. The prosecution's case was also hampered by suspicions that its star witness, Wilkinson, had turned on Burr to cover up his own involvement in a plot to seize western lands. On the stand, Wilkinson admitted that he had erased portions of the letter he'd sent Jefferson, and that these portions referred to Wilkinson's previous correspondence with Burr.

The jury found Burr not guilty.

Was Burr in fact a traitor? What he was planning to do in the West in 1805 and 1806 remains as contested and as murky as whether he conspired to seize the presidency in 1800. Certainly Burr continued to pursue some sort of western American dream. After his trial, he traveled to England, Sweden, and France, trying unsuccessfully to drum up foreign support for an expedition into Spanish territory.

It's unfair, however, to view Burr solely through Jefferson's eyes. Burr headed west in search of land and glory and without regard for diplomatic or legal niceties, but so did many other Americans, many of whom were hailed as heroes. Andrew Jackson seized Florida from Spain in 1818; Sam Houston took Texas in 1835; Winfield Scott and Zachary Taylor invaded Mexico in 1847. Jefferson himself bought Louisiana without giving any more consideration than

Spain or France to what its inhabitants wanted, and Jefferson sent Lewis and Clark across the continent, again without regard for foreign or native claims.

Burr returned to America in 1812 and lived long enough to see Houston seize Texas from Spain and declare an independent nation. "You see?" he exclaimed, according to a nineteenth-century biographer. "I was right! I was only thirty years too soon! What was treason in me thirty years ago, is patriotism now!"

THOMAS JEFFERSON

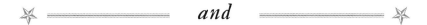 *and*

JOHN MARSHALL

The law is nothing more than an ambiguous text to be explained by his sophistry into any meaning which may subserve his personal malices.

THOMAS JEFFERSON ON JOHN MARSHALL

He is among the most ambitious, and I suspect among the most unforgiving of men. His great power is over the mass of the people and this power is chiefly acquired by professions of democracy. Every check on the wild impulse of the moment is a check on his own power.

JOHN MARSHALL ON THOMAS JEFFERSON

FOR THOMAS JEFFERSON, THE NOT-GUILTY VERDICT FOR Aaron Burr was all the more galling because the trial was presided over by John Marshall.

"By all rights," historian Joseph Ellis wrote, "Marshall should have been a Jeffersonian disciple." Other young Virginia revolutionaries, among them James Madison and James Monroe, fell under the sway of Thomas Jefferson during the Revolution and followed him to the presidency. Marshall, as Jefferson's second cousin, a legitimate war hero, and a brilliant lawyer, seemed similarly destined.

Instead, as chief justice of the Supreme Court, Marshall became the most formidable foe Jefferson faced during his two terms as president. The Jefferson-Marshall feud long outlasted Jefferson's feuds with Alexander Hamilton, who died in 1804, and with John Adams, with whom Jefferson ultimately resumed a close friendship. The Jefferson-Marshall feud was deeply personal but also, more than any other founding feud, a test of the balance of power between the branches of government the two men represented.

BIOGRAPHERS AND HISTORIANS HAVE TRIED TO TRACE JEFFERSON and Marshall's mutual dislike to a moment in their mutual background—without much success.

Marshall might have resented that Jefferson's side of the family was much wealthier than his, but he never said so. Jefferson might have resented that Marshall married the daughter of Rebecca Burwell, the woman Jefferson had unsuccessfully courted years before, but Jefferson never said so.

Marshall, along with George Washington and his troops,

suffered through the bitter winter at Valley Forge and may have had a soldier's contempt for Jefferson, who as governor of Virginia fled from Richmond and then from Monticello, when British troops approached. Again, though, this is pure speculation.

Their personalities and styles were radically different. Jefferson, despite his democratic politics, was aloof and aristocratic and preferred writing to speaking in public. Marshall, despite his fears of unchecked democracy, enjoyed everyone's company, whether they were fellow members of his club in Richmond or enlisted men at Valley Forge or even his political opponents (with the exception of Jefferson). Jefferson was a brilliant philosopher and a lousy lawyer. Marshall grounded much of his political thinking in the law and was extremely effective in the courtroom.

Whatever their personal differences, what ultimately made them enemies was politics. During the first decade of the republic, Republicans came to dominate Virginia politics. Jefferson, though a member of Washington's cabinet, became the de facto leader of the opposition Republican Party. Marshall was a Federalist, perhaps the most prominent one in Virginia besides Washington. In 1792, as Marshall considered running for Congress, Jefferson suggested to Madison that they redirect his ambitions. "I think nothing better could be done," Jefferson wrote, with words that would surely have haunted him if he later remembered them, "than to make him a judge." In 1795, Jefferson worried that Marshall's "lax lounging manners have made him popular."

Marshall's popularity soared in 1798 after he returned from

a mission to France. Marshall failed to reach an accord with the French government but was lauded, especially by Federalists, for taking a firm stand in the face of demands that included a bribe for the French foreign minister. In 1799, John Adams appointed Marshall secretary of state.

In the next year's presidential election, Jefferson defeated Adams but finished in a tie with Aaron Burr. This left the decision to the House of Representatives, which was still controlled by Federalists. Marshall saw Burr as a dangerous and unprincipled opportunist, but he still could not bring himself to support his cousin. When Marshall's fellow Federalist, Alexander Hamilton, explained how he had reluctantly come to prefer Jefferson to Burr, Marshall responded that Jefferson's pro-French bias "totally…unfit him for the chief magistracy of a nation which cannot indulge those prejudices without sustaining deep and permanent injury." Moreover, "the morals of the author of the letter to Mazzei cannot be pure." Here Marshall was referring to a 1796 letter Jefferson had written to a friend, in which he accused Federalists of favoring the British and of wanting to create a monarchy in America. When the letter found its way into various newspapers, Federalists, including Marshall, were indignant. Marshall concluded he could support neither Burr nor Jefferson.

Before Adams turned over the presidency to Jefferson, he made a number of last-minute appointments. The most significant was naming Marshall chief justice. This was the one grudge Jefferson had trouble letting go of when he and Adams were searching for ways to end their feud and renew their friendship.

Appointing Marshall chief justice meant he would administer the oath of office to Jefferson. This led to a somewhat tense exchange in which Jefferson and Marshall managed to agree on one thing: they would both arrive punctually.

Still, there was reason to hope they might be able to work together, or at least not against each other. Just before he administered the oath, Marshall speculated that Jefferson might not be as dangerous as Federalists feared. "The democrats are divided into speculative theorists and absolute terrorists," he wrote to Charles Cotesworth Pinckney. "With the latter I am not disposed to class Mr. Jefferson."

Jefferson's inaugural address buttressed hopes that his election would dampen partisan flames. He called on Federalists and Republicans alike to "unite with one heart and one mind" and to "restore to social intercourse that harmony and affection without which liberty, and even life itself, are but dreary things." Later that afternoon, Marshall finished his letter to Pinckney. He reported that the inaugural address was "well judged and conciliatory."

———◆◆◆◆———

Hopes for harmony did not last long.

Adams's last-minute appointments included forty-two justices of the peace for the District of Columbia. All were Federalists. Adams sent the commissions to Marshall, who was still his secretary of state. With so much else going on, Marshall neglected to deliver the commissions, and they were still sitting on a table in the State

Department when Jefferson took over as president and Madison took over as secretary of state. Jefferson, annoyed by Adams's efforts to saddle him with Federalist appointees, accepted twenty-five but told Madison to ignore the rest of the commissions.

Among those thus denied a job as justice of the peace was William Marbury, a Federalist businessman. Marbury sued Madison, and the case found its way in 1803 to the Supreme Court, where Marshall presided.

Marshall's decision in *Marbury v. Madison* was a work of genius. He was not prepared directly to confront Jefferson and the power of the presidency. Instead, he took on Congress, ruling that the law authorizing the Court to issue a writ compelling Madison to deliver the commission was unconstitutional. As a result, Marbury would not get his job and neither Jefferson nor Madison would have grounds to protest.

Yet Marshall also asserted that the Supreme Court—and not Jefferson or future presidents or the Congress—had the power to decide what was constitutional. "An act of the legislature repugnant to the Constitution is void," he wrote. "It is emphatically the province and duty of the judicial department to say what the law is."

The concept of judicial review—that the Court was the ultimate arbiter of what was and was not constitutional—was by no means new, but nor was it generally accepted. In *The Federalist*, Hamilton described the Supreme Court as "beyond comparison the weakest of the three departments of power." During the 1790s, the Supreme Court met only one month each year and didn't even have a set meeting place. Many assumed it was up to Congress to interpret the Constitution; after all, Congress had created the Bill of Rights, Congress had decided the federal government had the power to create a national bank, and Congress had limited the freedoms delineated in the First Amendment by passing the Alien and Sedition Acts. Many, including Jefferson, believed that if the people of the United States felt a law was unconstitutional, they could and should elect to Congress representatives who would change that law. Marshall's ruling in *Marbury v. Madison* set forth that the power of the Supreme Court was on a par with that of Congress—and the presidency.

Even more infuriating to Jefferson were Marshall's rulings in the 1807 trial of Jefferson's former vice president. After killing Hamilton in their duel and then fleeing west, Burr had gathered men and supplies on an island in the middle of the Ohio River owned by one of his followers, Harman Blennerhassett.

Back east, rumors circulated that Burr was not planning to attack Spanish territories, as he claimed, but rather to lead a western secession from the United States. Jefferson, convinced Burr had tried to steal the presidency from him, was predisposed to believe the worst. He was handed evidence of the worst in October 1806 in the form of a package from General James Wilkinson, commander of the United States forces in the West. It contained a letter, allegedly from Burr to Wilkinson, in which Burr discussed what sounded like a revolution in the West and offered to make the general his second in command. Jefferson ordered Burr arrested and sent a message to Congress declaring him guilty of treason. The treason trial took place in Richmond, where Marshall happened to be the circuit court judge.

The prosecution's case was hampered from the start by the dubious character of its star witness, Wilkinson. The general seemed to know a lot about Burr's plots, and many suspected he had turned on Burr to conceal his own involvement.

Still, Jefferson pushed on. The president had no formal role in the case but was very active behind the scenes, writing more than fifty letters to prosecutors. Jefferson must have hoped that for once he and Marshall might be on the same side, since Marshall disliked Burr as much as the president did.

Jefferson's hopes were crushed when Marshall ruled that treason required an "overt act." That meant prosecutors had to prove Burr took part in the military actions on Blennerhassett's island. And prosecutors had to concede that, at the time his forces gathered on the island, Burr was a day's journey away. Whatever plot Burr had in mind—and historians and biographers continue to debate this—it did not constitute treason, as Marshall defined it. A day after Marshall's ruling, the jury found Burr not guilty.

For Marshall, the verdict confirmed that no one, including the president, was above the law, and that everyone, even someone as detestable as Burr, was entitled to the protection of the law. If the government were allowed to hang Burr (and that was the punishment for treason), then, as Marshall wrote in one of his rulings on the case, "the hand of malignity may grasp any individual against whom its hate may be directed." Jefferson must have suspected it was his hand Marshall had in mind.

For Jefferson, the case confirmed that the chief justice saw himself as the law. "We had supposed we possessed fixed laws to guard us equally against treason and oppression," Jefferson fumed. "But it now appears we have no law but the will of the judge."

———◆·◆·◆———

AFTER BURR WAS FOUND NOT GUILTY, JEFFERSON PUSHED Congress to make changes to the court system. Jefferson hoped, for example, that Congress would give itself the power to remove federal judges from office. The proposals went nowhere, since most congressmen did not question the Supreme Court's power. Jefferson's protégés and successors, Madison and Monroe, accepted the Court as a legitimate and equal branch of the federal government.

Not Jefferson. Long after he retired, he continued to rage against Marshall and the Court. Unlike the Congress or the president, the judges were not elected; to Jefferson, this made them as dangerously undemocratic as Federalists or monarchists. Marshall was even more dangerous than Hamilton, since he acted under cover of the law.

In 1810, Jefferson bemoaned to future president John Tyler that "we have long enough suffered under the…prostitution of law to party passions in one judge." That same month he grumbled to Madison that Marshall's "twistifications in the case of Marbury, in that of Burr…show how dexterously he can reconcile law to his personal biases." To the newspaper editor Thomas Ritchie in 1820, he described the judiciary as "the subtle corps of sappers and miners constantly working underground to undermine the foundations of our confederated fabric."

To Joseph Story, who served on the Supreme Court with Marshall, Jefferson supposedly explained:

When conversing with Marshall I never admit anything. So sure as you admit any position to be good, no matter how remote from the conclusion he seeks to establish, you are gone. So great is his sophistry you must never give him an affirmative answer or you will be forced to grant his conclusion. Why, if he were to ask me if it were daylight or not, I'd reply, "Sir, I don't know, I can't tell."

The Supreme Court withstood all of Jefferson's attacks, so perhaps Marshall should have the final word here. This is from an 1821 letter from Marshall to Story:

For Mr. Jefferson's opinion as respects this department it is not difficult to assign the cause. He is among the most ambitious, and I suspect among the most unforgiving of men. His great power is over the mass of the people and this power is chiefly acquired by professions of democracy. Every check on the wild impulse of the moment is a check on his own power, and he is unfriendly to the source from which it flows. He looks, of course, with ill will at an independent judiciary.

THOMAS JEFFERSON

 *and*

JOHN RANDOLPH

The old Republican Party is already ruined, past redemption.

JOHN RANDOLPH

The example of John Randolph, now the outcast of the world, is a caution to all honest and prudent men, to sacrifice a little of self-confidence, and to go with their friends, although they may sometimes think they are going wrong.

THOMAS JEFFERSON

TO JOHN MARSHALL AND OTHER FEDERALISTS, THOMAS JEFFERSON was too much of a Republican. To John Randolph, a distant cousin of Jefferson's, he was not nearly enough of one.

While Jefferson led the opposition, Randolph already tended to take stronger stands against the growth of federal power. When John Adams signed the Alien and Sedition Acts, for example, Jefferson drafted resolutions arguing that states had the right to ignore federal laws they considered unconstitutional. This was certainly a strange situation: Jefferson was making the case for dissolving the union of which he was then vice president. But Jefferson took this position in secret, and his weapons, typically, were words. Randolph went further: he openly advocated arming opponents of the acts.

When Jefferson became president, Randolph was at first pleased and proud to be a part of his party, as the Republicans cut taxes, abolished judgeships the Federalists had created, and reduced the national debt. Randolph was an effective, if eccentric, party leader, rounding up support for presidential initiatives ranging from the Louisiana Purchase to judicial reform. William Plumer, a Federalist from New Hampshire, described Randolph at work: "Mr. Randolph goes to the House booted and spurred, with his whip in his hand," Plumer wrote, "in imitation, it is said, of members of the British Parliament… The Federalists ridicule and affect to despise him; but a despised foe often proves a dangerous enemy."

Jefferson recognized Randolph was a useful ally, later writing that his "popular eloquence gave him such advantages as to place him unrivaled as the leader of the House." Many followed Randolph's lead, despite his impatience with those who disagreed with him and his temper or, as Jefferson put it, the "humiliations he subjected them to." Randolph, too, later looked back on Jefferson's first years as president as "brilliant."

Tensions between Jefferson and Randolph surfaced publicly in 1805. Ten years earlier, the Georgia legislature had transferred to four companies more than 35 million acres known as the Yazoo land, after one of the tract's major rivers. It was a blatantly corrupt deal. Every legislator who voted for it had been bribed with shares in the land companies, and in 1796 every one of those legislators was voted out of office. The problem was that in the interim the companies had sold shares to many innocent investors.

A federal commission consisting of three members of Jefferson's cabinet, including Secretary of State James Madison, recommended that the federal government purchase the land and pay the investors a fraction of their claims. Neither Madison nor Jefferson thought this the ideal solution, but it made the best of a bad situation.

Randolph did not believe in compromise. He saw the federal government as usurping Georgia's land and rights.

"What is the spirit against which we now struggle, and which we have vainly endeavored to stifle?" he asked the House of Representatives in January 1805 with his characteristic drama—or melodrama. "A monster generated by fraud, nursed in corruption, that in grim silence awaits his prey."

Randolph expected this of Federalists, he continued, but he was appalled by the willingness of Republicans to go along with the deal. "Of what consequence is it that a man smiles in your face, holds out his hand and declares himself the advocate of those political principles to which you are also attached," Randolph demanded to know, "when you see him acting with your adversaries upon other principles, which the voice of the nation has put down, which I did hope were buried, never to rise again in this section of the globe?"

Randolph's influence was enough to kill the Yazoo deal. Jefferson "did not know what course to pursue with Mr. Randolph," he confided to John Smith, a senator from Ohio. According to Smith, the president complained Randolph "would never consult him—or his friends," and would "pursue his own course," even when "wild and impracticable."

The breach between Jefferson and Randolph widened in February 1805, when Randolph led the effort to impeach Supreme Court Justice Samuel Chase. Jefferson and Randolph were on the same side here—both were appalled by Chase's efforts to push a Federalist agenda from the bench. In March, the Senate acquitted Chase. Jefferson blamed Randolph, rightly, for bungling the prosecution; John Quincy Adams, who was a senator from Massachusetts at the time of the trial, described Randolph's arguments during the trial:

> *[They are] without order, connection, or argument; consisting altogether of the most hackneyed commonplaces of popular declamation, mingled up with panegyrics and invectives upon persons, with a few well-expressed ideas, a few striking figures, much distortion of face and contortion of body, tears, groans, and sobs, with occasional pauses for recollection, and continual complaints of having lost his notes.*

Randolph, for his part, blamed Jefferson and Madison for pushing privately but not publicly for the impeachment.

The full break came in December 1805, when Jefferson confidentially requested that Congress appropriate $2 million to buy Florida from Spain. To Randolph, the idea of secret negotiations, whether over Yazoo or Florida, smacked of corruption. Randolph again frustrated Jefferson's plans, this time by rallying opposition to the tax that would have financed the Florida purchase.

By then, Randolph was openly advocating a third party. Moderation, Randolph explained, was "the mask which ambition has worn" throughout history.

Randolph became the leader of the Tertium Quids—from the Latin *tertium quid*, a "third something." The Quids saw themselves as neither Federalists nor Republicans. The Republican Party was "past redemption," Randolph wrote. "New men and new maxims are the order of the day." The Quids saw Jefferson as an apostate, a Federalist posing as a Republican while embracing the federal power that was now his.

"I came here prepared to cooperate with the government in all its measures," Randolph declared. "I found I might cooperate, or be an honest man."

Jefferson liked to dismiss Randolph as irrelevant. "The defection of so prominent a leader threw [the House of Representatives] into dismay and confusion for a moment," he wrote Wilson Cary Nicholas, "but they soon rallied to their own principles." Randolph was, Jefferson wrote James Monroe, headed toward "a state of as perfect obscurity as if his name had never been known."

But there was no question that Randolph's attacks bothered

Jefferson. After Randolph published an essay setting forth his objections to the Florida deal, Jefferson complained, albeit privately, about the "bold and unauthorized assertions."

Among those Randolph insulted in the House of Representatives was his fellow congressman, Thomas Mann Randolph, who was John Randolph's cousin and Jefferson's son-in-law. Thomas Mann Randolph felt he had no choice but to challenge John Randolph to a duel. Jefferson's advice to his son-in-law revealed how little he thought of John Randolph:

> *How different is the stake which you two would bring into the field! On his side, unentangled in the affections of the world, a single life, of no value to himself or others. On yours, yourself, a wife, and a family of children, all depending for all their happiness and protection in this world on you alone.*

Tempers cooled, and the duel was never fought. (Not surprisingly, John Randolph's words often led others to consider a challenge, and in 1826 he and Henry Clay exchanged shots. Both missed.)

JEFFERSON'S PREDICTION THAT RANDOLPH WAS HEADED toward a state of perfect obscurity turned out to be true. Randolph's positions were too extreme and his behavior too idiosyncratic to attract a large following. Randolph tried to persuade

Monroe to oppose Madison in the 1808 presidential election, but Monroe correctly perceived that his clearest path to the White House was to back Madison and wait his turn. The Quids were an annoyance but never mounted a serious challenge to Jefferson or Madison.

By 1811, Jefferson could gloat that Randolph was an "outcast" and "a caution to all honest and prudent men, to sacrifice a little of self-confidence, and to go with their friends, although they may sometimes think they are going wrong."

In 1813, his own constituents voted Randolph out of office, partly because of his opposition to the war with England. He was replaced by John W. Eppes, another son-in-law of Jefferson. Randolph retired to his plantation, the appropriately named Bizarre.

Randolph won back his seat in 1815. More surprisingly, he ultimately found himself on the same side as Jefferson, at least when it came to the great debate of the period. Both Randolph and Jefferson opposed the Missouri Compromise—Clay's plan that Missouri be admitted to the union as a slave state and Maine as a free state, with slavery to be prohibited in all states formed north of a designated line and allowed in all states formed south of the line. Both Randolph and Jefferson feared the debate over slavery would ultimately doom the union.

Randolph called slavery a "cancer," but for once he cautioned against radicalism, in this case the radicalism of abolitionists. "When men are furiously and fanatically fond of any object, of any set of opinions whatever, they will sacrifice to that fanatical attachment, their own property, their own peace, their own lives," Randolph told Congress. "Fanaticism, political or religious, has no stopping place short of heaven—or of hell."

The Missouri Compromise, Jefferson agreed, was a "reprieve only." To hold slaves, he famously wrote, was to "have the wolf by the ears, and we can neither hold him, nor safely let him go. Justice is in one scale, and self-preservation in the other."

Neither Jefferson nor Randolph could imagine a world where the liberties they fought for and about could be extended to slaves. Here, sadly, they found the common ground on which they could end their feud. In 1824, Jefferson even went so far as to list Randolph, along with Madison and Monroe, among his "companions in sentiments…all good men and true."

THOMAS JEFFERSON

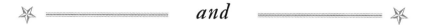 *and*

PHILLIS WHEATLEY

Religion...has produced a Phyllis Whately [sic]; but it could not produce a poet. The compositions published under her name are below the dignity of criticism.

THOMAS JEFFERSON

THOMAS JEFFERSON AND PHILLIS WHEATLEY DID NOT FEUD, AT LEAST IN the way of others in this book. They never met, never corresponded. As an enslaved and then a freed black woman living in Boston, Wheatley could not have reasonably expected Jefferson to associate with her, even as an adversary. But Wheatley's poetry was such a challenge to Jefferson's views on the capabilities of Africans that he felt the need to discredit it. And though Wheatley herself was in no position to respond, others did, and in doing so shaped the debate over slavery and race long after Jefferson and Wheatley were dead.

WHEATLEY'S ENCOUNTERS WITH THREE OTHER FOUNDERS WERE more personal and more satisfying than that with Jefferson.

Wheatley met John Hancock in October 1772. He was one of the self-designated "most respectable characters in Boston" who had agreed to interrogate Wheatley in order to determine whether she had actually written the poems attributed to her.

Susanna Wheatley, the wife of a Boston merchant, had bought a seven-year-old girl in July 1761, when the slave ship *Phillis* (hence her name) docked. By the time she was eight, with the help of Susanna's daughter, she had learned to read. By the time she was twelve, she was writing poems. By the time she was sixteen, her poem about the evangelical preacher George Whitefield had been widely circulated in the colonies and in England and had made her famous.

Susanna Wheatley recognized that this was someone extraordinary, and she decided to collect the poems in a book. She tried to gather subscribers to pay for the publication, but she couldn't find enough people who believed a slave girl could have written these poems. So Susanna Wheatley arranged the meeting with Hancock and seventeen fellow luminaries. After the meeting, Hancock added his signature (not quite as prominently as it would later appear on the Declaration of Independence) to the following "attestation":

We whose names are underwritten do assure the world that the poems...were (as we verily believe) written by Phillis, a young Negro girl, who was but a few years since brought an uncultivated barbarian from Africa and has ever since been, and now is, under the disadvantage of serving as a slave in a family in this town. She has been examined by some of the best judges and is thought qualified to write them.

Insulting as this might seem to modern readers, for an enslaved woman in 1773 it was high praise. Yet even with the attestation of the city's most respectable characters, Susanna still could not find a publisher in Boston. She found one in London, where she traveled along with Phillis, and it was there that Phillis met Benjamin Franklin.

Wheatley's meeting with Franklin was briefer than with Hancock. Franklin described it in a letter to his cousin, Jonathan Williams:

Upon your recommendation I went to see the black poetess and offered her any services I could do her. Before I left the house, I understood her master was there and had sent her to me but did not come into the room himself, and I thought was not pleased with the visit. I should perhaps have enquired first for him; but I had heard nothing of him. And I have heard nothing since of her.

The master Franklin referred to was Nathanael Wheatley, Susanna's son. Some historians have speculated that Nathanael was not nearly as rude as Franklin implied, and that Franklin seized on the alleged slight to cut short the visit. Franklin was in England as a representative of several colonies, and any publicity about his visit with Wheatley might very well have focused on the hypocrisy of

Americans' demands for British rights and liberties while owning slaves. By neither ignoring Wheatley completely nor providing her with any real support, Franklin made sure commentators had little to comment on. A longer meeting might have been personally as well as politically awkward, since, until 1781, Franklin himself owned slaves.

Susanna and her family recognized the hypocrisy of their position, and on their return to Boston freed Phillis. So it was as a free woman, in October 1775, that Wheatley sent to George Washington her poem marking his appointment as commander of the Continental Army. The poem's final stanza reads:

> Proceed, great chief, with virtue on thy side,
> Thy ev'ry action let the goddess guide.
> A crown, a mansion, and a throne that shine,
> With gold unfading, Washington! be thine.

Washington wrote back in February 1776. He apologized for the delay, explaining he had been busy, and thanked her for "the elegant lines you enclosed…a striking proof of your great poetical talents." Washington added that he would have arranged for the poem to be published but feared that, "while I only meant to give the world this new instance of your genius, I might have incurred the imputation of vanity."

Modesty did not stop Washington from forwarding the poem to his former secretary, Joseph Reed. Reed took the hint and sent the poem to the *Virginia Gazette*. The *Gazette* published the poem and others republished it.

The Wheatley-Washington correspondence may have had more than literary significance. A month before Washington received Wheatley's poem, he had barred black men from the Continental Army. Two months after he received the poem, he issued the order that allowed freed black men (but not slaves) to enlist.

Wheatley must have been further encouraged by praise her poems generated from other Enlightenment and Revolutionary figures, among them Benjamin Rush and John Paul Jones in America and Voltaire in France. But the greatest American contributor to the Enlightenment was soon to deliver the most vituperative attack on Wheatley's poetry.

———◆•✕•◆———

In *Notes on the State of Virginia*, written in 1781 and published in 1785, Thomas Jefferson wrote:

> *Among the blacks is misery enough, God knows, but no poetry... Their love is ardent, but it kindles the senses only, not the imagination. Religion, indeed, has produced a Phyllis Whately [sic]; but it could not produce a poet. The compositions published under her name are below the dignity of criticism.*

Jefferson's attack on Wheatley was part of a broader attack on her race. He described black people, in *Notes*, as incapable of reason or art. Lest there be any doubt that their deficiencies were innate and not a result of their condition, Jefferson explained that some Roman slaves were great artists, but "they were of the race of whites."

It was not that Jefferson liked slavery. "The whole commerce between master and slave is a perpetual exercise of the most boisterous passions, the most unremitting despotism on the one part, and degrading submissions on the other," he wrote in *Notes*. "And can the liberties of a nation be thought secure when we have removed their only firm basis, a conviction in the minds of the people that these liberties are of the gift of God?" Jefferson hoped eventually to see "the slave rising from the dust, his condition mollifying…under the auspices of heaven, for a total emancipation."

But black people could only be freed if they were also expelled from America. "Why not retain and incorporate the blacks into the state, and thus save the expense of supplying, by importation of white settlers, the vacancies they will leave?" Jefferson asked. His answer:

> *Deep-rooted prejudices entertained by whites; ten thousand recollections, by the blacks, of the injuries they have sustained; new provocations; the real distinctions which nature has made; and many other circumstances, will divide us into parties, and produce convulsions which will probably never end but in the extermination of the one or the other race.*

Notes catalogued "the real distinctions which nature has made": blacks were ugly, they smelled bad, they could not create art...or poetry. Hence, Wheatley's poetry was not poetry at all.

Jefferson's *Notes* provided slave owners, historian David Grimsted wrote, with "superior intellectual camouflage." They could continue to love liberty and to hold slaves, because America's leading spokesman for liberty had determined that the Negro race was inherently inferior. Jefferson's thoughts on race were widely quoted throughout the South. John Burk, for example, cited Jefferson in 1804 to argue that slaveholders, "while they wish to vindicate the liberty of human nature, are anxious also to preserve its dignity and beauty."

Wheatley could not respond. Unable to find a publisher for a second collection of her poems, she had lived her final years in poverty and died in 1784, the year before Jefferson's *Notes* was first published.

But the *Notes* inspired the writings of not only slave owners but also abolitionists, the latter eager to refute Jefferson's arguments. The writer Gilbert Imlay, in 1792, quoted Wheatley at length so that readers would have "an opportunity...of estimating her genius and Mr. Jefferson's judgment." Imlay was confident that "Phillis appears much the superior."

African Americans were especially committed to challenging Jefferson's racism. The antislavery activist David Walker, in 1829, urged his fellow black men to buy a copy of Jefferson's *Notes* to give to their children. "For let no one of us suppose," Walker wrote "that the refutations which have been written by our white friends are enough… We, and the world wish to see the charges of Mr. Jefferson refuted by the blacks themselves."

Jefferson's comments, wrote the critic Henry Louis Gates Jr., "became the strongest motivation for blacks to create a body of literature that would implicitly prove Jefferson wrong." Gates went so far as to say: "If Phillis Wheatley was the mother of African American literature, there is a sense in which Thomas Jefferson can be thought of as its midwife."

Ironically, among modern critics, Wheatley's most vehement detractors have been African Americans. Many have criticized her for the very trait for which Hancock and his fellow judges had once praised her: her mastery of neoclassical—i.e., white—conventions. Amiri Baraka, the poet and critic, wrote that Wheatley's "pleasant imitations of eighteenth-century English poetry are far and, finally, ludicrous departures from the huge black voices that splintered southern nights." Critics also attacked her for embracing the Revolution and Christianity—the cause and the religion of slaveholders.

But, as Gates and others have pointed out, Wheatley's patriotic poems can be read as not only a call for America's freedom but also for the freedom of enslaved people. Her prose left even less room for misinterpretation. "In every human breast," Wheatley wrote in a letter to Samson Occom, an Indian who had been ordained as a minister, "God has implanted a principle, which we call love of freedom; it is impatient of oppression, and pants for deliverance." In the same letter, Wheatley made clear what she thought of American slaveholders who complained about British tyranny: "How well the cry for liberty, and the reverse disposition for the exercise of oppressive power over others agree,—I humbly think it does not require the penetration of a philosopher to determine."

Wheatley's writings did not dislodge Jefferson's prejudices, but they did force other founders, including Hancock and Washington and Rush and Jones, to reconsider some of their views. "The African American poet who seems a prisoner of eighteenth-century conventions wrote for the Revolutionary present and the American future," wrote historian David Waldstreicher. "In doing so she made the Revolution that much more revolutionary."

JOHN ADAMS

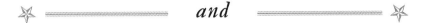

and

MERCY OTIS WARREN

His prejudices and his passions were sometimes too strong for his sagacity and judgment.

MERCY OTIS WARREN ON JOHN ADAMS

If Mrs. Warren is determined to be enrolled in the glorious list of libelers of John Adams, she is welcome...
But most of these have already come to a bad end, and the rest will follow.

JOHN ADAMS

JOHN ADAMS WAS DEEPLY AND UNDENIABLY COMMITTED TO THE American Revolution. He was equally committed to making sure future generations would appreciate his role in it. He would not stand for anyone who interfered with either commitment.

In 1809, Adams wrote a series of essays in the *Boston Patriot* devoted in large part to answering the charges made in the 1800 "Letter from Alexander Hamilton, Concerning the Public

Conduct and Character of John Adams, Esq., President of the United States." Adams had no qualms about attacking Hamilton, but his true motive was to defend his own reputation; after all, the election Hamilton had hoped to influence with his letter was eight years in the past, and Hamilton had been dead for four years. Adams's lengthy correspondence with Thomas Jefferson was also intended in large part to secure Adams's proper place in history.

So it should come as no surprise that Adams read with great interest Mercy Otis Warren's sweeping *History of the Rise, Progress, and Termination of the American Revolution*, published between 1805 and 1807. Also unsurprising was Adams's deep distress that, of the more than thirteen hundred pages in Warren's three volumes, only four were devoted to him. Worse, those four pages were hardly complimentary: among the flaws for which Warren criticized Adams were his "pride of talents and much ambition" and after the Revolution developing "a partiality for monarchy."

Adams felt personally as well as politically betrayed, since he had been Mercy Warren's good friend and a longtime supporter of her literary work. His enraged letters to Warren and her indignant replies fill hundreds of pages.

———— ◆◈◆ ————

SOON AFTER THE BOSTON TEA PARTY, ADAMS WROTE HIS FELLOW revolutionary James Warren. Adams wanted the Tea Party "celebrated by a certain poetical pen, which has no equal." The pen he had in mind was that of Warren's wife Mercy.

Mercy Warren obliged, penning "The Squabble of the Sea Nymphs." Adams quickly arranged for the poem's publication in the *Boston Gazette* and described it to James Warren as "one of the most incontestable evidences of real genius."

In 1775, James Warren sent Adams the first two acts of Mercy Warren's play, *The Group*, in which she satirized Parliament's efforts to limit popular representation in the Massachusetts legislature. "Of all the geniuses which have yet arisen in America," Adams wrote Mercy Warren, "there has been none, superior, to one, which now shines... I know of none, ancient or modern, which has reached the tender, the pathetic, the keen and severe, and at the same time the soft, the sweet, the amiable, and the pure, in greater perfection."

Adams was no feminist. "It was best for a general rule that the fair should be excused from the arduous cares of war and state," he wrote James Warren. But, Adams continued, Mercy Warren and his own wife Abigail "ought to be exceptions, because I have ever ascribed to those ladies, a share and no small one neither, in the conduct of our American affairs."

Mercy Warren, too, generally accepted a traditional woman's role. She stayed very much in the shadows of her husband and of her brother James Otis. Otis was an early advocate for the rights of Americans; Adams credited him with coining the revolutionary rallying cry that "taxation without representation was tyranny." Alas, by the 1770s, Otis had gone insane, possibly because of a blow to his head during a brawl with a British customs official. His sister took over some of his correspondence, and this may have opened her mind to the possibility of writing for a broader audience.

Even then, she depended on Adams for news of what was going on at the Continental Congress and for encouragement. He provided both. The Adams home in Quincy, Massachusetts, was a bit too far from the Warrens' home in Plymouth for regular visits, but the couples corresponded regularly and occasionally dined together. Mercy Warren responded with poems, plays, and essays satirizing the British position in Massachusetts. In 1774, Adams, quoting a seventeenth-century theologian, wrote her that his pen, when compared to hers, "conscious of its inferiority, falls out of my hand." On learning that Warren had stopped work on her history of the Revolution, Abigail Adams in 1777 expressed her distress that Warren would "give up so important a service."

The friendship began to cool after the Revolution, as Adams moved to Europe for various diplomatic posts and as James Warren joined Anti-Federalists in opposing those who, like Adams, believed the nation needed a new constitution with a stronger federal government. In a 1788 pamphlet, Mercy Warren made the Anti-Federalist case. The Constitution was, she wrote, a "many-headed monster; of such motley mixture, that its enemies cannot trace a feature of democratic or republican extract; nor have its friends the courage to denominate it a monarchy, an aristocracy, or an oligarchy." Warren was especially appalled by the lack of a bill of rights. She saw America as following in the footsteps of the

Roman republic-turned-empire, its once virtuous citizens seduced by power and wealth.

The Adams-Warren friendship was further strained in 1789 when Adams was elected vice president. Warren appealed to him to find a job for her husband, whose Anti-Federalism had antagonized former allies in Massachusetts, and for her son, Winslow, who was deeply in debt. Adams replied that such patronage was beyond his power, since appointments were up to the president and not the vice president. Moreover, Adams said, referring to Warren's opposition to the Constitution: "General Warren did differ for a time from all his friends and did countenance measures that appear to me, as they did to those friends, extremely pernicious." Adams added, somewhat sanctimoniously, that even if he had the power to give a job to James or Winslow, it would "belie the whole course of my public and private conduct and all the maxims of my life, if I should ever consider public authority entrusted to me to be made subservient to my private views, or those of my family or friends."

Warren and Adams continued to exchange polite but prickly letters. When Adams became president in 1796, Warren congratulated him but couldn't resist insinuating he had attained his dream of a crown. Abigail responded on John's behalf, writing that the only crown to which she aspired was "in a country where envy can never enter to plant thorns beneath it."

Abigail was justified in suggesting the Warrens envied the Adamses. John and Abigail had become president and first lady, while James's political career and Mercy's literary one had floundered. But Mercy was certainly not the only one to accuse John Adams of coveting a crown. Adams's presidency was consumed by partisan attacks. His Republican opponents accused him of abandoning republican principles by supporting England rather than France and plotting to go to war against the latter; by creating a standing army; and by signing into law the Sedition Act, which allowed Federalists, while they were in power, to prosecute newspaper editors who criticized the government. When Jefferson defeated Adams in the presidential election of 1800, Adams returned to Quincy, feeling misunderstood and unappreciated.

<hr />

THE FIRST VOLUME OF WARREN'S *HISTORY* APPEARED IN 1805 AND the third in 1807. It was this last volume that included her critique of Adams and his presidency.

"Mr. Adams was undoubtedly a statesman of penetration and ability," Warren began, "but his prejudices and his passions were sometimes too strong for his sagacity and judgment."

She then brought up his postwar mission to England, where "unfortunately for himself and his country, he became so enamored with the British constitution, and the government, manners, and laws of the nation, that a partiality for monarchy appeared, which was inconsistent with his former professions of republicanism." After returning to America, "he was implicated by a large portion of his countrymen, as having relinquished the republican system, and forgotten the principles of the American Revolution, which he had advocated for near twenty years."

What had "beclouded" Adams's principles? "It may…be charitably presumed," Warren concluded, "that by living long near the splendor of courts and courtiers…he might become so biased in his judgment as to think that a hereditary monarchy was the best government for his native country."

Jefferson wrote a polite note to Warren, saying he had "no doubt the work she has prepared will be equally useful to our country and honorable to herself." That must have been satisfying to Warren as she waited, nervously, for the response of Jefferson's predecessor as president. Then came the barrage.

Adams's first letter was dated July 11, 1807. He wrote, he coldly explained, to note several errors, so she might correct them in any future edition. She had said his passions and prejudices were too strong for his sagacity and judgment. He asserted:

I am not conscious of having ever in my life taken one public step or performed one public act from passion or prejudice or from any other motive than the public good. If I had acted from passion or prejudice, from interest, ambition, or avarice, the public affairs of this country would have been in a much less prosperous condition than they are, and my private fortune, both in rank and property, much more enviable than it is.

As for her claim that he had developed a partiality for monarchy, Adams explained he despised any form of tyranny, whether it was "absolute monarchy" or "absolute democracy." He had therefore "always advocated a mixed elective government in three branches," so that there would be a balance of power. He considered a limited monarchy appropriate for England, but for Americans he "would not recommend…either a hereditary king or a hereditary nobility."

In letter after letter, Adams spewed forth his frustrations with how Warren misunderstood him, and how he feared posterity would as well.

He denied her characterization of him as prideful and ambitious with great vehemence and at great length, apparently unaware that in doing so he was proving her point. "I have done more labor, run through more and greater dangers, and made greater sacrifices than any man among my contemporaries, living or dead, in the service of my country," he asserted.

Increasingly irate and rambling, he turned threatening: "Most of these [who have libeled Adams] have already come to a bad end, and the rest will follow." Mostly, he was indignant. "What have I done," he cried out, "to merit so much malevolence from a lady concerning whom I never in my life uttered an unkind word or a disrespectful insinuation?"

Warren tried to placate Adams. "Angry as you have appeared in your late correspondence," she wrote him, "your integrity or industry, your moral or religious character, has never been impeached; and, when the impartiality of history required any observation on political delinquency, your change of opinion has been imputed to the dictates of conscience, which may sometimes be misguided where there are the best intentions."

But, despite a lifetime habit of deference, she did not retract anything, nor did she apologize. "I have uniformly endeavored to write with impartiality, to state facts correctly, and to draw characters with truth and candor, whether the friends or the foes of my country, or the enemies of myself and family, or of those connected by the dearest ties of nature and friendship."

Eventually, an exasperated Warren suggested that his stream of complaints was fed by his vanity. "Had not Mr. Adams been suffering under suspicions that his fame had not been sufficiently attended to," she wrote, "he would not have put such a perverse construction on every passage where he is named."

There was no point in further discussion, she concluded. "The history has gone forth to the world, with my settled and fixed determination to disregard its censure or applause. Mr. Adams's opinions might have defeated this determination, had they not have been so marked with passion, absurdity, and inconsistency as to appear… like the ravings of a maniac."

His tenth letter and her sixth letter ended the correspondence— and the relationship—for several years.

In 1812, Warren, then a widow in her eighties, reached out to John Adams in letters to Abigail Adams and to a mutual friend,

Elbridge Gerry. Abigail Adams responded warmly and sent Warren a lock of her hair entwined with "that of your ancient friend's, at his request"—indicating John, too, was willing to put their feud behind them.

Not entirely, however. Adams could not restrain himself from complaining to Gerry about errors in Warren's book. "History," he told Gerry, "is not the province of the ladies."

★ ★ ★

EPILOGUE

JEFFERSON, AS ANY READER OF THIS BOOK (OR OF ANY OTHER BOOK about him) will have noticed, feuded with many of his fellow founders. How did he manage to antagonize so many?

His critics, then and now, have attributed it to Jefferson's hypocrisy. He was our greatest proponent of liberty, yet he owned slaves. He fought the growth of federal power until he became president, after which he did not hesitate to wield all the power that came with the office. Even if one grants that Jefferson changed his positions because circumstances changed, his chameleon-like behavior would still have earned the enmity of those whose positions Jefferson abandoned.

To his detractors, Jefferson was a chameleon in another sense as well: his machinations were often difficult to spot. He pretended not to care about politics while using others, such as Madison, to achieve his ends. He presented himself as a philosopher and writer, not a politician. When he wrote his own epitaph, he asked to be remembered for three achievements: writing the Declaration of

Independence, writing Virginia's statute for religious freedom, and founding the University of Virginia. Not a word about his years in politics or as president, despite the fact that, as his biographer Jon Meacham concluded, "the closest thing to a constant in his life was his need for power and control."

Jefferson's flaws infuriated many and sparked many a feud. The same is true for his fellow founders. Adams was as vain as Hamilton claimed, and Hamilton was as ambitious as Adams feared. These qualities made them enemies with each other and with others. The founders could be petty, their feuds very personal.

Yet there was more to the founders and their feuds than that. The founders fought with each other, too, because they understood that at stake was the future of the nation, indeed the future of their great republican experiment. They believed, as Paine proclaimed, that "the birthday of a new world is at hand"—and they were right.

"Despite all his shortcomings and all the inevitable disappointments and mistakes and dreams deferred," Meacham wrote of Jefferson, "he left America, and the world, in a better place than it had been when he first entered the arena of public life." The same could be said of America's other founding fathers and mothers. Their ideas and their actions created the United States.

So, too, did their feuds.

Though the founders did not fully grasp it, democracy depends on differences of opinion. From the founders' feuds—sometimes philosophical, sometimes political, sometimes petty—emerged a nation more democratic than the founders envisioned.

American politics today could certainly benefit from more civility. Politicians ought not to follow in the footsteps of Aaron Burr and Alexander Hamilton and start shooting each other. But Americans ought also not to yearn for a time when everyone agreed about everything. That time never existed.

Despite John Adams's reminiscence, thirteen clocks never struck as one—nor should we want them to do so.

★ ★ ★

NOTES

PREFACE

ix   "Thirteen clocks…" John Adams to H. Niles, 13 February 1818, in *The Works of John Adams, Second President of the United States: With a Life of the Author, Notes and Illustrations*, vol. 10, ed. Charles Francis Adams (Boston: Little, Brown, 1856), 283.

ix   "to brave the storm…" John Dickinson's Notes for a Speech in Congress, 1 July 1776, in *Letters of Delegates to Congress, 1774–1789*, vol. 4, *May 16–August 15, 1776*, ed. Paul H. Smith (Washington, DC: Library of Congress, 1979), 352.

x   "a perfection of mechanism…" Adams to Niles in Charles Francis Adams, *Works of John Adams*, 10:283.

x   "The progress of evolution…" *The Education of Henry Adams: An Autobiography* (Boston: Houghton Mifflin, 1918), 266.

xi   "the governor of the ancient dominion…" [Alexander Hamilton], "Phocion—No. IX," *Gazette of the United States, & Philadelphia (PA) Daily Advertiser*, 25 October, 1796.

xi   "a man whose history…" Thomas Jefferson to George Washington, 9 September 1792, in Oberg and Looney, *Papers of Jefferson Digital*

Edition, http://rotunda.upress.virginia.edu/founders/TSJN-01–24 –02–0330.

xi   "the revolution of 1800..." Thomas Jefferson to Spencer Roane, 6 September 1819, in *The Writings of Thomas Jefferson*, vol. 15, ed. Andrew A. Lipscomb (Washington, DC: Thomas Jefferson Memorial Association, 1903), 212.

xii   "the disgusting egotism..." Letter from Alexander Hamilton, Concerning the Public Conduct and Character of John Adams, Esq. President of the United States, [24 October 1800], in *The Papers of Alexander Hamilton*, vol. 25, *July 1800–April 1802*, ed. Harold C. Syrett (New York: Columbia University Press, 1977), 196.

xii   "an insolent coxcomb" and "a bastard brat..." John Adams to Benjamin Rush, 25 January 1806, in *The Spur of Fame: Dialogues of John Adams and Benjamin Rush, 1805–1813*, ed. John A. Schutz and Douglass Adair (San Marino, CA: Huntington Library, 1966), 48.

xii   "Men who have been intimate..." Thomas Jefferson to Edward Rutledge, 24 June 1797, in Oberg and Looney, *Papers of Jefferson Digital Edition*, http://rotunda.upress.virginia.edu/founders/TSJN -01-29-02-0357.

xii   "a pure unadulterated logocracy" As reprinted in *Salmagundi; or, the Whim-Whams and Opinions of Launcelot Langstaff, Esq. and Others*, vol. 1 (New York, 1814), 159.

xiii   "The American experiment..." H. Michael Hartoonian, Richard D. Van Scotter, and William E. White, *The Idea of America: How Values Shaped Our Republic and Hold the Key to Our Future* (Williamsburg, VA: Colonial Williamsburg Foundation, 2013), 9.

DEANE AND LEE

1   "His countenance is disgusting…" John Adams to James Lovell, 21 September 1779, in *Papers of John Adams*, vol. 8, *March 1779–February 1780*, ed. Gregg L. Lint et al. (Cambridge, MA: Belknap Press of Harvard University Press, 1989), 165.

1   "What Mr. Deane's political principles…" Samuel Adams to Samuel Cooper, 3 January 1779, in *The Writings of Samuel Adams*, vol. 4, ed. Harry Alonzo Cushing (New York: Octagon Books, 1968), 112.

2   "his judgment of men…" John Adams to Lovell in Lint, *Papers of John Adams*, 8:165.

4   "must be shaved and bled" Silas Deane to Edward Bancroft, [8 January 1778], in *Collections of the New-York Historical Society for the Year 1887: The Deane Papers*, vol. 2, *1777–1778*, Publication Fund Series 20 (New York: New-York Historical Society, 1888), 310.

4   "my pity of your sick mind…" Benjamin Franklin to Arthur Lee, 3 April 1778, in *The Papers of Benjamin Franklin*, vol. 26, *March 1 through June 30, 1778*, ed. William B. Willcox (New Haven: Yale University Press, 1987), 223.

4   "Deane had misapplied…" Worthington Chauncey Ford, ed., *Journals of the Continental Congress, 1774–1789*, vol. 12, *1778: September 2–December 31* (Washington, DC: Government Printing Office, 1908), 927.

5   "I certify that if my zeal…" Pierre-Augustin Caron de Beaumarchais to Congress, 23 March 1778, in *For the Good of Mankind: Pierre-Augustin Caron de Beaumarchais Political Correspondence Relative*

to the American Revolution, trans. and ed. Antoinette Shewmake (Lanham, MD: University Press of America, 1987), 299.

5   "a faithful, active, and able minister..." Benjamin Franklin to Henry Laurens, 31 March 1778, in Willcox, *Papers of Franklin*, 26:204.

5   "applied one shilling..." "Silas Deane's Narrative, Read before Congress," 21 December 1778, in *Collections of the New-York Historical Society for the Year 1888: The Deane Papers*, vol. 3, *1778–1779*, Publication Fund Series 21 (New York: New-York Historical Society, 1889), 197.

6   "their ears have been shut..." Silas Deane, *Pennsylvania Packet or the General Advertiser* (Philadelphia), 5 December 1778.

6   "barbarous, unmanly, and unsupported attack..." Thomas Paine, *Pennsylvania Packet or the General Advertiser* (Philadelphia), 15 December 1778.

6   "the ruin of Mr. Deane..." John Adams, diary entry, 8 February 1779, in *Diary and Autobiography of John Adams*, vol. 2, ed. L. H. Butterfield (Cambridge, MA: Belknap Press of Harvard University Press, 1961), 345.

6   "party disputes and personal quarrels..." George Washington to Benjamin Harrison, 18 December 1778, in *The Papers of George Washington Digital Edition*, ed. Theodore J. Crackel (Charlottesville: University of Virginia Press, Rotunda, 2008), http://rotunda.upress .virginia.edu/founders/GEWN-03–18–02–0510.

7   "What Mr. Deane's political principles..." Samuel Adams to Cooper in Cushing, *Writings of Samuel Adams*, 4:112.

7   "To what a degree of corruption..." Thomas Paine, *Pennsylvania Packet or the General Advertiser* (Philadelphia), 12 January 1779.

7 "I do not conceive…" Robert Morris, *Pennsylvania Packet or the General Advertiser* (Philadelphia), 9 January 1779.

8 "immoral" and "the doctor is old…" Richard Henry Lee to Arthur Lee, 16 September 1778, in *Letters of Delegates to Congress, 1774–1789*, vol. 10, *June 1–September 30, 1778*, ed. Paul H. Smith (Washington, DC: Library of Congress, 1983), 652. Some words in this letter, including "immoral" and some in the following phrase, were originally written in code.

8 "We ought to inquire…" Silas Deane to Simeon Deane, 16 May 1781, in *Royal Gazette* (New York), November 10, 1781.

9 "You believe that…" Silas Deane to Benjamin Franklin, 13 May 1782, in Cohn, *Papers of Franklin*, 37:365.

WASHINGTON AND WASHINGTON

11 "I do hereby…" Proclamation by John Murray, fourth Earl of Dunmore, 7 November 1775, National Archives, London, England, CO 5/1353, no. 335.

12 "If…that man is not crushed…" George Washington to Richard Henry Lee, 26 December 1775, in Crackel, *Papers of Washington Digital Edition*, http://rotunda.upress.virginia.edu/founders/GEWN-03–02–02–0568.

12 "there is not a man of them…" and "Liberty is sweet" Lund Washington to George Washington, 3 December 1775, in Crackel, *Papers of Washington Digital Edition*, http://rotunda.upress.virginia.edu/founders/GEWN-03–02–02–0434.

14 "without…carrying away…" Preliminary Articles of Peace, November

30, 1782, in *Treaties and Other International Acts of the United States of America*, vol. 2, *Documents 1–40: 1776–1818*, ed. Hunter Miller (Washington, DC: Government Printing Office, 1931), 99.

14 "several of my own…" George Washington to Benjamin Harrison, 30 April 1783, in *The Writings of George Washington from the Original Manuscript Sources, 1745–1799*, vol. 26, *January 1, 1783–June 10, 1983*, ed. John C. Fitzpatrick (Washington, DC: Government Printing Office, 1938), 370.

14 "the delivery of all Negroes…," "upwards of 6,000…," "what appeared to him…," and "It could not have been the intention…" "Substance of a Conference between General Washington and Sir Guy Carleton," 6 May 1783, in Fitzpatrick, *Writings of Washington*, 26:402–404.

15 "Delivering up the Negroes…" Ibid., 404.

15 "Harry Washington, 43…" Graham Russell Hodges, ed., *The Black Loyalist Directory: African Americans in Exile after the American Revolution* (New York: Garland Publishing, 1996), 111–112.

16 "By freeing his slaves…" Ron Chernow, *Washington: A Life* (New York: Penguin Press, 2010), 802.

LINCOLN AND SHAYS

19 "Your resources are few…" Benjamin Lincoln to George Washington [Benjamin Lincoln's address to Daniel Shays, 30 January 1787], 4 December 1786[–4 March 1787], in *The Papers of George Washington Digital Edition*, ed. Theodore J. Crackel (Charlottesville: University of Virginia Press, Rotunda, 2008), http://rotunda.upress .virginia.edu/founders/GEWN-04-04-02-0374-0002.

20   "When rightly understood…" George Richards Minot, *The History of the Insurrections, in Massachusetts, in the Year MDCCLXXXVI, and the Rebellion Consequent Thereon* (Worcester, MA, 1788), iv.

21   "this disposition of the people…" Ibid., 12.

21   "shed their blood…" Ibid., 17.

21   "headed by one Daniel Shays" Ibid., 48.

22   "People were diverted…" Lincoln to Washington, 4 December 1786[–4 March 1787], in Crackel, *Papers of Washington Digital Edition*.

23   "Your resources are few…" Ibid.

23   "accommodation of our present unhappy affairs" Ibid.

24   "In monarchies…" William V. Wells, *The Life and Public Services of Samuel Adams, Being a Narrative of His Acts and Opinions, and of His Agency in Producing and Forwarding the American Revolution. With Extracts from His Correspondence, State Papers, and Political Essays*, vol. 3 (Boston: Little, Brown, 1865), 246.

24   "a few prompt examples" Benjamin Lincoln to Henry Knox, 17 February 1787, the Gilder Lehrman Collection, the Gilder Lehrman Institute of American History, New York, NY, GLC02437.03456, transcript retrieved from http://www.gilder lehrman.org/collections.

25   "the suppression of…" George Washington to Benjamin Lincoln, 23 March 1787, in Crackel, *Papers of Washington Digital Edition*, http://rotunda.upress.virginia.edu/founders/GEWN-04–05 –02–0099.

25   "generalissimo" Black List for Hampshire County, Massachusetts Historical Society, Boston, MA, as reproduced in *In Debt of Shays:*

The Bicentennial of an Agrarian Rebellion, ed. Robert A. Gross (Charlottesville: University Press of Virginia, 1993), 41.

25 "I at their head..." and "I never had any appointment..." C. O. Parmenter, *History of Pelham, Mass., from 1738 to 1898, Including the Early History of Prescott* (Amherst, MA: Carpenter & Morehouse, 1898), 396, 397.

HENRY AND MADISON

27 "I smelt a rat" Hugh Blair Grigsby, *The History of the Virginia Federal Convention of 1788, with Some Account of the Eminent Virginians of That Era Who Were Members of the Body*, vol. 1, ed. R. A. Brock (Richmond: Virginia Historical Society, 1890), 32.

28 "Even more than the Lincoln-Douglas debate..." Joseph J. Ellis, *American Creation: Triumphs and Tragedies at the Founding of the Republic* (New York: Alfred A. Knopf, 2007), 120.

28 "in a voice of thunder..." William Wirt, *Sketches of the Life and Character of Patrick Henry* (Philadelphia, 1817), 65.

28 "His imagination was copious..." Thomas Jefferson's Notes on Patrick Henry, [before 12 April 1812], in The Papers of Thomas Jefferson Digital Edition, ed. Barbara Oberg and J. Jefferson Looney (Charlottesville: University of Virginia Press, Rotunda, 2008), http://rotunda.upress.virginia.edu/founders/TSJN 03–04 02–0495–0003.

28 "all tongue..." Thomas Jefferson to George Rogers Clark, 26 November 1782, in Oberg and Looney, *Papers of Jefferson Digital Edition*, http://rotunda.upress.virginia.edu/founders/TSJN-01–06 –02–0193.

29 "bill for establishing…" "A Bill for Establishing Religious Freedom," in Oberg and Looney, *Papers of Jefferson Digital Edition*, http://rotunda.upress.virginia.edu/founders/TSJN-01–02–02–0132 –0004–0082.

29 "While Mr. Henry lives…" Thomas Jefferson to James Madison, 8 December 1784, in Oberg and Looney, *Papers of Jefferson Digital Edition*, http://rotunda.upress.virginia.edu/founders/TSJN-01–07 –02–0402.

29 "You give me a credit…" James Madison to William Cogswell, 10 March 1834, Founders Online, National Archives, http://founders .archives.gov/documents/Madison/99–02–02–2952.

30 "the best commentary…" Thomas Jefferson to James Madison, 18 November 1788, in Oberg and Looney, *Papers of Jefferson Digital Edition*, http://rotunda.upress.virginia.edu/founders/TSJN-01–14 –02–0062.

30 "I smelt a rat" Grigsby, *History of the Virginia Federal Convention of 1788*, 1:32.

30 "the best that could be obtained…" George Washington to Benjamin Harrison [and Patrick Henry and General Thomas Nelson], 24 September 1787, in Crackel, *Papers of Washington Digital Edition*, http://rotunda.upress.virginia.edu/founders/GEWN-04–05 –02–0316.

30 "I have to lament…" Patrick Henry to George Washington, 19 October 1787, in Crackel, *Papers of Washington Digital Edition*, http:// rotunda.upress.virginia.edu/founders/GEWN-04–05–02–0350.

30 "I conceive the Republic…" *The Documentary History of the*

Ratification of the Constitution, vol. 9, *Ratification of the Constitution by the States: Virginia [2]*, ed. John P. Kaminski and Gaspare J. Saladino (Madison: State Historical Society of Wisconsin, 1990), 929–930.

30   "What right had they to say…" Ibid., 930.

31   "Disorders have arisen…" Ibid., 931.

31   "The powers of the federal government…" Ibid., 996.

31   "Twenty-three years ago…" Ibid., 952.

32   "When the American spirit…" Ibid., 959.

32   "He tells you of important blessings…" *The Documentary History of the Ratification of the Constitution*, vol. 10, *Ratification of the Constitution by the States: Virginia [3]*, ed. John P. Kaminski and Gaspare J. Saladino (Madison: State Historical Society of Wisconsin, 1993), 1506.

32   "a violent storm arose…" Ibid., 1506.

33   "rising on the wings…" Wirt, *Sketches of the Life and Character of Patrick Henry*, 296.

34   "Although the form of government…" Patrick Henry to James Monroe, 24 January 1791, in *The Papers of James Monroe: Selected Correspondence and Papers*, vol. 2, *1776–1794*, ed. Daniel Preston (Westport, CT: Greenwood Press, 2006), 493.

34   "I have bid adieu…" Patrick Henry to George Washington, 16 October 1795, in *Patrick Henry: Life, Correspondence, and Speeches*, vol. 2, ed. William Wirt Henry (1891; repr., New York: Burt Franklin, 1969), 558–559.

34   "one of the richest ironies…" Ellis, *American Creation*, 125.

HAMILTON AND JEFFERSON

35   "A man whose history…" Thomas Jefferson to George Washington, 9
      September 1792, in *The Papers of Thomas Jefferson Digital Edition*,
      ed. Barbara B. Oberg and J. Jefferson Looney (Charlottesville:
      University of Virginia Press, Rotunda, 2008), http://rotunda
      .upress.virginia.edu/founders/TSJN-01–24–02–0330.

35   "If…the people of the United States…" An American [Alexander
      Hamilton], *Gazette of the United States* (Philadelphia), August
      4, 1792.

36   "if some of its defects…" Thomas Jefferson to Benjamin Rush, 16
      January 1811, in Oberg and Looney, *Papers of Jefferson Digital
      Edition*, http://rotunda.upress.virginia.edu/founders/TSJN-03
      –03–02–0231.

36   "with its existing vices…" Ibid.

36   "my trinity of the three greatest men…" Ibid.

36   "The greatest man…" Ibid.

36   "Tired at length…" "Objections and Answers Respecting the
      Administration of the Government" (enclosure), Alexander
      Hamilton to George Washington, 18 August 1792, in *The Papers of
      Alexander Hamilton*, vol. 12, *July 1792–October 1792*, ed. Harold
      C. Syrett (New York: Columbia University Press, 1967), 252.

37   "The governor of the ancient dominion…" Phocion [Alexander
      Hamilton], "Phocion—No. IX," *Gazette of the United States, &
      Philadelphia (PA) Daily Advertiser* (Philadelphia), 25 October 1796.

38   "I was persuaded…" "Jefferson's Account of the Bargain on the
      Assumption and Residence Bills," [1792?], in Oberg and Looney,

Papers of Jefferson Digital Edition, http://rotunda.upress.virginia .edu/founders/TSJN-01–17–02–0018–0012.

40   "their happiness and their safety..." An American [Alexander Hamilton], *Gazette of the United States* (Philadelphia), 4 August 1792.

40   "an engine in the hands..." "Notes on the Letter of Christoph Daniel Ebeling," [after October 15, 1795], in Oberg and Looney, *Papers of Jefferson Digital Edition*, http://rotunda.upress.virginia.edu/founders /TSJN-01–28–02–0391.

40   "from the present republican..." Thomas Jefferson to George Washington, 23 May 1792, in Oberg and Looney, *Papers of Jefferson Digital Edition*, http://rotunda.upress.virginia.edu/founders /TSJN-01–23–02–0491.

40   "The idea of introducing..." "Objections and Answers," in Syrett, *Papers of Hamilton*, 12:251.

40   "furnish the singular spectacle..." "Final Version of an Opinion on the Constitutionality of an Act to Establish a Bank," 23 February 1791, in *The Papers of Alexander Hamilton*, vol. 8, *February 1791– July 1791*, ed. Harold C. Syrett (New York: Columbia University Press, 1965), 98.

40   "suffer...the slanders..." Jefferson to Washington in Oberg and Looney, *Papers of Jefferson Digital Edition*.

41   "national government transformed..." and "have ever aimed..." An American [Alexander Hamilton], *Gazette of the United States* (Philadelphia), 4 August 1792.

41   "ruin and devastation..." [Alexander Hamilton], "The French

Revolution," [1794], in *The Papers of Alexander Hamilton*, vol. 17, *August 1794–December 1794*, ed. Harold C. Syrett (New York: Columbia University Press, 1972), 586.

41 "Of all the events…" Stanley Elkins and Eric McKitrick, *The Age of Federalism: The Early American Republic, 1788–1800* (New York: Oxford University Press, 1993), 77.

42 "daily pitted in the cabinet…" Thomas Jefferson to Walter Jones, 5 March 1810, in Oberg and Looney, *Papers of Jefferson Digital Edition*, http://rotunda.upress.virginia.edu/founders/TSJN-03–02 –02–0223.

42 "I believe the views…" George Washington to Thomas Jefferson, 18 October 1792, in Oberg and Looney, *Papers of Jefferson Digital Edition*, http://rotunda.upress.virginia.edu/founders/TSJN-01–24 –02–0464.

42 "All personal and partial considerations…" Alexander Hamilton to unknown recipient, 8 November 1796, in *The Papers of Alexander Hamilton*, vol. 20, *January 1796–March 1797*, ed. Harold C. Syrett (New York: Columbia University Press, 1974), 377.

42 "The passions are too high…" Thomas Jefferson to Edward Rutledge, 24 June 1797, in Oberg and Looney, *Papers of Jefferson Digital Edition*, http://rotunda.upress.virginia.edu/founders/TSJN-01–29 –02–0357.

43 "Every difference of opinion…" Thomas Jefferson, First Inaugural Address, 4 March 1801, in Oberg and Looney, *Papers of Jefferson Digital Edition*, http://rotunda.upress.virginia.edu/founders/TSJN -01–33–02–0116–0004.

ADAMS AND JEFFERSON

45   "That you and I differ…" Thomas Jefferson to John Adams, 17 July
      1791, in *The Papers of Thomas Jefferson Digital Edition*, ed. Barbara
      B. Oberg and J. Jefferson Looney (Charlottesville: University of
      Virginia Press, Rotunda, 2008), http://rotunda.upress.virginia.edu
      /founders/TSJN-01–20–02–0076–0009.

45   "His mind is now poisoned…" John Adams to Abigail Adams, 6
      January 1794, in *My Dearest Friend: Letters of Abigail and John
      Adams*, ed. Margaret A. Hogan and C. James Taylor (Cambridge,
      MA: Belknap Press, 2007), 348.

46   "obnoxious" "Autobiography," in *The Works of John Adams, Second
      President of the United States: With a Life of the Author, Notes and
      Illustrations*, vol. 2, ed. Charles Francis Adams (Boston: Little,
      Brown, 1850), 515.

46   "the odd couple…" Joseph J. Ellis, *Founding Brothers: The
      Revolutionary Generation* (New York: Alfred A. Knopf,
      2000), 163.

46   "My new partner…" John Adams to Arthur Lee, 31 January 1785,
      in *Papers of John Adams*, vol. 16, *February 1784–March 1785*, ed.
      Gregg L. Lint et al. (Cambridge, MA: Belknap Press of Harvard
      University Press, 2012), 510.

46   "to leave behind me…" Abigail Adams to Thomas Jefferson, 6 June
      1785, in *The Adams-Jefferson Letters: The Complete Correspondence
      between Thomas Jefferson and Abigail and John Adams*, ed. Lester
      J. Cappon (Chapel Hill, NC: University of North Carolina Press,
      1959, 1988), 28.

46 "vain" and "irritable" and "as disinterested as the being…" Thomas Jefferson to James Madison, 30 January 1787, in Oberg and Looney, *Papers of Jefferson Digital Edition*, http://rotunda.upress.virginia .edu/founders/TSJN-01–11–02–0095.

47 "tempted to have kept…" Abigail Adams to Thomas Jefferson, 6 July 1787, in Cappon, *Adams-Jefferson Letters*, 183.

47 "His Highness…" *Journal of William Maclay: United States Senator from Pennsylvania, 1789–1791*, ed. Edgar S. Maclay (New York: D. Appleton, 1890), 25–26.

47 "the most superlatively ridiculous…" and "Always an honest man…" Thomas Jefferson to James Madison, 29 July 1789, in Oberg and Looney, *Papers of Jefferson Digital Edition*, http://rotunda.upress .virginia.edu/founders/TSJN-01–15–02–0307.

48 "Mankind found by experience…" "Discourses on Davila. No. 32," *Gazette of the United States* (Philadelphia), 27 April 1791.

48 "something is at length…" Thomas Jefferson to Jonathan B. Smith, 26 April 1791, in Oberg and Looney, *Papers of Jefferson Digital Edition*, http://rotunda.upress.virginia.edu/founders/TSJN-01–20 –02–0076–0002.

48 "The friendship and confidence…" and "That you and I differ…" Jefferson to John Adams in Oberg and Looney, *Papers of Jefferson Digital Edition*.

49 "Jefferson went off yesterday…" John Adams to Abigail Adams in Hogan and Taylor, *My Dearest Friend*, 348.

49 "filled with glory…" and "various little incidents…" Thomas Jefferson to John Adams, 28 December 1796, in Oberg and Looney, *Papers*

of Jefferson Digital Edition, http://rotunda.upress.virginia.edu
/founders/TSJN-01–29–02–0190–0002.

50   "I am his junior…" Thomas Jefferson to James Madison, 1 January
       1797, in Oberg and Looney, *Papers of Jefferson Digital Edition,*
       http://rotunda.upress.virginia.edu/founders/TSJN-01–29–02
       –0196–0002.

50   "There may be real embarrassments…" James Madison to Thomas
       Jefferson, 15 January 1797, in Oberg and Looney, *Papers of Jefferson
       Digital Edition,* http://rotunda.upress.virginia.edu/founders/TSJN
       -01–29–02–0206.

51   "I consider these laws…" Thomas Jefferson to Stevens Thomson
       Mason, 11 October 1798, in Oberg and Looney, *Papers of Jefferson
       Digital Edition,* http://rotunda.upress.virginia.edu/founders/TSJN
       -01–30–02–0375.

51   "between Adams, war, and beggary…" [James Thomson Callender],
       The Prospect before Us, vol. 1 (Richmond, VA, 1800), 167.

51   "You who are for French…" *Daily Advertiser* (New York City), 28
       April 1800.

52   "The grand question…" *Gazette of the United States, and Daily
       Advertiser* (Philadelphia), 11 September 1800.

52   "the revolution of 1800…" Thomas Jefferson to Spencer Roane,
       6 September 1819, in *The Writings of Thomas Jefferson,* vol. 15,
       ed. Andrew A. Lipscomb (Washington, DC: Thomas Jefferson
       Memorial Association, 1903), 212.

53   "mutual esteem" and "personal displeasure" Thomas Jefferson to Abigail
       Adams, 13 June 1804, in Cappon, *Adams-Jefferson Letters,* 270.

54   "the lowest and vilest slander…," "severed the bonds…," and "The serpent you cherished…" Abigail Adams to Thomas Jefferson, 1 July 1804, in Cappon, *Adams-Jefferson Letters*, 273, 274.

54   "A letter from you…" Thomas Jefferson to John Adams, 21 January 1812, in Oberg and Looney, *Papers of Jefferson Digital Edition*, http://rotunda.upress.virginia.edu/founders/TSJN-03–04 –02–0334.

55   "As we had been longer…" Thomas Jefferson to John Adams, 27 June 1813, in Cappon, *Adams-Jefferson Letters*, 336.

55   "You and I ought not to die…" John Adams to Thomas Jefferson, 15 July 1813, in Cappon, *Adams-Jefferson Letters*, 358.

55   "We acted in perfect harmony…" Thomas Jefferson to John Adams, 28 October 1813, in Cappon, *Adams-Jefferson Letters*, 391–392.

ADAMS AND HAMILTON

57   "I have read his heart…" Abigail Adams to John Adams, 28 January 1797, Adams Family Papers: An Electronic Archive, Massachusetts Historical Society, http://www.masshist.org/digitaladams/archive /doc?id=L17970128aa&bc=%2Fdigitaladams%2Farchive%2F browse%2Fletters_1796_1801.php.

57   "A vanity without bounds…" Letter from Alexander Hamilton, Concerning the Public Conduct and Character of John Adams, Esq. President of the United States, [24 October 1800], in *The Papers of Alexander Hamilton*, vol. 25, *July 1800–April 1802*, ed. Harold C. Syrett (New York: Columbia University Press, 1977), 195.

58   "disturb the harmony…" Alexander Hamilton to Theodore Sedgwick,

[9 November 1788], in *The Papers of Alexander Hamilton*, vol. 5, *June 1788–November 1789*, ed. Harold C. Syrett (New York: Columbia University Press, 1962), 231.

58   "the most insignificant…" John Adams to Abigail Adams, 19 December 1793, in *The Adams Papers Digital Edition*, ed. C. James Taylor (Charlottesville: University of Virginia Press, Rotunda), 2008–2015, http://rotunda.upress.virginia.edu/founders/ADMS-04-09 –02–0278.

58   "heir apparent" John Adams to Abigail Adams, 20 January 1796, Adams Family Papers: An Electronic Archive, Massachusetts Historical Society, http://www.masshist.org/digitaladams/archive /doc?id=L17960120ja.

59   "a temper far more discreet…" Letter from Hamilton, Concerning the Conduct and Character of Adams, in Syrett, *Papers of Hamilton*, 25:195.

59   "Beware of that spare…" Abigail Adams to John Adams, Adams Family Papers.

60   "At present…" John Adams to James McHenry, 22 October 1798, in *The Works of John Adams, Second President of the United States: With a Life of the Author, Notes and Illustrations*, vol. 8, ed. Charles Francis Adams (Boston: Little, Brown, 1858), 613.

60   "one of the wildest extravagances…" "Mr. Adams's Correspondence Continued," *Boston Patriot*, 7 June 1809.

60   "By some he is considered…" George Washington to John Adams, 25 September 1798, in *The Papers of George Washington Digital Edition*, ed. Theodore J. Crackel (Charlottesville: University of

Virginia Press, Rotunda, 2008), http://rotunda.upress.virginia.edu
/founders/GEWN-06–03–02–0015.

61   "If I should consent…" John Adams to Oliver Wolcott (unsent), 24
      September 1798, in Charles Francis Adams, *Works of John Adams*,
      8:603–604n1.

61   "began to indulge…" Ron Chernow, *Alexander Hamilton* (New York:
      Penguin Press, 2004), 566.

62   "If the chief is too desultory…" Alexander Hamilton to James
      McHenry, 27 June 1799, in *The Papers of Alexander Hamilton*,
      vol. 23, *April 1799–October 1799*, ed. Harold C. Syrett (New
      York: Columbia University Press, 1976), 227.

62   "That man…" Abigail Adams to William S. Smith, 7 July 1798, as
      quoted in Alexander DeConde, *The Quasi-War: The Politics and
      Diplomacy of the Undeclared War with France 1797–1801* (New
      York: Charles Scribner's Sons, 1966), 97.

62   "with such agitation…" "Mr. Adams's Correspondence Continued,"
      Boston Patriot, 10 May 1809.

63   "the greatest intriguant…" James McHenry to John Adams, 31 May
      1800, in *The Papers of Alexander Hamilton*, vol. 24, *November
      1799–June 1800*, ed. Harold C. Syrett (New York: Columbia
      University Press, 1976), 557.

63   "the most splendid diamond…" John Adams to James Lloyd, 6
      February 1815, in *The Works of John Adams, Second President of
      the United States: With a Life of the Author, Notes and Illustrations*,
      vol. 10, ed. Charles Francis Adams (Boston: Little, Brown,
      1856), 115.

63   "If we must have an enemy…" Alexander Hamilton to Theodore
      Sedgwick, 10 May 1800, in Syrett, *Papers of Hamilton*, 24:475.

64   "It has been repeatedly mentioned…" Alexander Hamilton to John
      Adams, 1 August 1800, in Syrett, *Papers of Hamilton*, 25:51.

64   "an extended tantrum in print" Chernow, *Alexander Hamilton*, 623.

64   "an imagination sublimated…" Letter from Hamilton, Concerning
      the Conduct and Character of Adams, in Syrett, *Papers of
      Hamilton*, 25:190.

65   "the disgusting egotism…" Ibid., 196.

65   "revolution of 1800" Thomas Jefferson to Spencer Roane, 6
      September 1819, in *The Writings of Thomas Jefferson*, vol. 15,
      ed. Andrew A. Lipscomb (Washington, DC: Thomas Jefferson
      Memorial Association, 1903), 212.

65   "Although I…suffered to pass…" John Adams to Benjamin
      Rush, 25 January 1806, in *The Spur of Fame: Dialogues of John
      Adams and Benjamin Rush, 1805–1813*, ed. John A. Schutz
      and Douglass Adair (San Marino, CA: Huntington Library,
      1966), 48.

PAINE AND WASHINGTON

67   "And as to you, sir…" Thomas Paine, *A Letter to George Washington,
      on the Subject of the Late Treaty Concluded Between Great-Britain
      and the United States of America, Including Other Matters* (London,
      1797), 32.

67   "is fortunate to get off…" Thomas Jefferson to James Madison, 8
      January 1797, in *The Papers of Thomas Jefferson Digital Edition*,

ed. Barbara B. Oberg and J. Jefferson Looney (Charlottesville: University of Virginia Press, Rotunda, 2008), http://rotunda .upress.virginia.edu/founders/TSJN-01–29–02–0200.

67 "the Foundingest Father…" Joseph J. Ellis, *His Excellency: George Washington* (New York: Alfred A. Knopf, 2004), xiv.

68 "I have often thought…" George Washington to Joseph Reed, 14 January 1776, in *The Papers of George Washington Digital Edition*, ed. Theodore J. Crackel (Charlottesville: University of Virginia Press, Rotunda, 2008), http://rotunda.upress.virginia.edu/founders /GEWN-03–03–02–0062.

68 "We have it in our power…" Thomas Paine, *Common Sense; Addressed to the Inhabitants of America…* (Philadelphia, 1776), 47.

68 "is working a powerful change…" George Washington to Joseph Reed, 1 April 1776, in Crackel, *Papers of Washington Digital Edition*, http://rotunda.upress.virginia.edu/founders/GEWN-03 –04–02–0009.

69 "These are the times…" [Thomas Paine], *The American Crisis*, No. 1 (Norwich, CT, 1776), 1.

69 "unabated fortitude" [Thomas Paine], *The American Crisis*, No. 5, *Addressed to General Sir William Howe* (Lancaster, PA; repr. Hartford, CT, 1778), 15.

70 "That his *Common Sense*…" George Washington to Richard Henry Lee, 12 June 1784, in Crackel, *Papers of Washington Digital Edition*, http://rotunda.upress.virginia.edu/founders/GEWN-04 –01–02–0307.

70 "extremely pleased to find…" Thomas Paine, *Rights of Man: Being*

an Answer to Mr. Burke's Attack on the French Revolution, 2nd ed. (Philadelphia, 1791), 4.

71 "running into extremes" George Washington to Lafayette, 18 June 1788, in Crackel, *Papers of Washington Digital Edition*, http://rotunda.upress.virginia.edu/founders/GEWN-04–06–02–0301.

71 "Let it suffice…" George Washington to Thomas Paine, 6 May 1792, in Crackel, *Papers of Washington Digital Edition*, http://rotunda.upress.virginia.edu/founders/GEWN-05–10–02–0225.

71 "I should be tempted…" Thomas Paine to James Monroe, 13 October 1794, in *Life and Writings of Thomas Paine*, ed. Daniel Edwin Wheeler (New York: Vincent Parke, 1908), 140–141.

72 "winked at his imprisonment…" James Monroe to James Madison, 5 July 1796, in *The Papers of James Madison Digital Edition*, ed. J. C. A. Stagg (Charlottesville: University of Virginia Press, Rotunda, 2010), http://rotunda.upress.virginia.edu/founders/JSMN-01–16–02–0247.

72 "The character which Mr. Washington…" Paine, *Letter to Washington*, 20.

73 "treacherous in private friendship…" Ibid., 32.

73 "It has some time been known…" Ibid., 7.

73 "Had it not been…" Ibid., 4–5.

73 "absolute falsehoods" George Washington to David Stuart, 8 January 1797, in *The Writings of George Washington from the Original Manuscript Sources, 1745–1799*, vol. 35, *March 30, 1796–July 31, 1797*, ed. John C. Fitzpatrick (Washington, DC: Government Printing Office, 1940), 359.

73   "He is in our textbooks…" Richard Brookhiser, *Founding Father: Rediscovering George Washington* (New York: The Free Press, 1996), 4.

74   "you might expect…" Letter to the Editor, *Columbian Centinel* (Boston), January 18, 1797.

74   "first in war…" Henry Lee, *A Funeral Oration, on the Death of General Washington…* (Philadelphia: 1800), 16.

75   "Not for the world…" Thomas Jefferson to Benjamin Waterhouse, 19 July 1822, in *Memoirs, Correspondence, and Private Papers of Thomas Jefferson, Late President of the United States*, vol. 4, Thomas Jefferson Randolph (London: Henry Colburn and Richard Bentley, 1829), 362.

75   "In the comic-book version…" Jill Lepore, "The Sharpened Quill," *The New Yorker*, October 16, 2006, 168, 170.

GRISWOLD AND LYON

77   "I called him a scoundrel…" Roger Griswold to unknown correspondent, 25 February 1798, W. G. Lane Collection, Sterling Memorial Library, Yale University, New Haven, CT, box 4, box 15/1798.

78   "He spoke loud enough…," 7 Annals of Congress 961 (1798).

78   "acted in opposition…" Ibid.

78   "if he should go into Connecticut…" Ibid.

78   "If you go into Connecticut…" Ibid.

79   "I did not think it my duty…" Ibid., 1027.

79   "if he fought them…" and "Mr. Lyon spat…" Ibid., 962.

80   "tended to degrade..." Ibid., 975.

80   "as citizens removed impurities..." Ibid., 1007.

80   "be disqualified for polite society" Ibid., 998.

80   "As soon as I saw...," "very much bruised," and "blood running..." Griswold to unknown correspondent.

81   "Against his will..." "Lyon and Griswold: Battle of the Wooden Sword" ([Rutland, VT?: Printed by Josiah Fay?, 1798]).

82   "spent a great part..." 7 Annals of Cong. 235 (1797).

82   "a mere beast..." Griswold to unknown correspondent.

83   "there was American blood enough..." 7 Annals of Cong. 232 (1797).

83   "Conquest had led..." Ibid., 235.

84   "write, print, utter, or publish..." An Act in Addition to the Act, Entitled "An Act for the Punishment of Certain Crimes against the United States," approved 14 July 1798, in *The Public Statutes at Large of the United States of America, from the Organization of the Government in 1789, to March 3, 1845...*, vol. 1, ed. Richard Peters (Boston: Charles C. Little and James Brown, 1845), 596.

84   "an unbounded thirst..." Francis Wharton, *State Trials of the United States during the Administrations of Washington and Adams* (Philadelphia: Carey and Hart, 1849), 333.

85   "a union of the northern states," "democracy is making...," and "there can be no safety..." Roger Griswold to Oliver Wolcott, 11 March 1804, in *Documents Relating to New-England Federalism, 1800–1815*, ed. Henry Adams (New York: Burt Franklin, [1969], originally published in Boston 1877), 355, 356.

COBBETT AND PAINE

87   "He has done all the mischief…" [William Cobbett], *An Antidote for Tom Paine's Theological and Political Poison…* (Philadelphia, 1796), 49.

87   "begin the world over again" Thomas Paine, *Common Sense; Addressed to the Inhabitants of America, on the Following Interesting Subjects…* (Philadelphia, 1776), 47.

88   "begotten by a wild boar…" John Adams to Benjamin Waterhouse, 29 October 1805, in *Statesman and Friend: Correspondence of John Adams with Benjamin Waterhouse, 1784–1822*, ed. Worthington Chauncey Ford (Boston: Little, Brown, 1927), 31.

88   "How Tom gets a living…" and "Whether his carcass…" Cobbett, *Antidote for Paine's Poison*, 48, 49.

88   "Thomas's having merited death…" Ibid., 36.

89   "It is hardly necessary…" Thomas Jefferson to John Taylor, 4 June 1798, in *The Papers of Thomas Jefferson Digital Edition*, ed. Barbara B. Oberg and J. Jefferson Looney (Charlottesville: University of Virginia Press, Rotunda, 2008), http://rotunda.upress.virginia .edu/founders/TSJN-01–30–02–0280.

90   "any false, scandalous and malicious…" An Act in Addition to the Act, Entitled "An Act for the Punishment of Certain Crimes Against the United States," in Richard Peters, ed., *The Public Statutes at Large of the United States of America, from the Organization of the Government in 1789, to March 3, 1845…* (Boston: Charles C. Little and James Brown, 1845), 596.

91   "Instead of that perfect freedom…" *Cobbett's Weekly Political Register*

8, no. 15 (12 October 1805) in *Cobbett's Political Register*, vol. 8, *From July to December, 1805* (London, 1805), 548.

91   "absolutely worse…" Cobbett, *Antidote for Paine's Poison*, 20.

91   "The most dangerous arguments…" William Cobbett, "Selections from Porcupine's Gazette, from July, 1799, to January, 1800," in *Porcupine's Works; Containing Various Writings and Selections, Exhibiting a Faithful Picture of the United States of America…*, vol. 11, (London, 1801), 95.

91   "infidel anarchist" Ibid., 4.

91   "a brutal and savage…" William Cobbett, "Life of Thomas Paine, Interspersed with Remarks and Reflections," in *Porcupine's Works; Containing Various Writings and Selections, Exhibiting a Faithful Picture of the United States of America…*, vol. 4 (London, 1801), 79.

91   "He had enjoyed partial revolts…" William Cobbett, "Political Censor, No. 4" in *Porcupine's Works; Containing Various Writings and Selections, Exhibiting a Faithful Picture of the United States of America…*, vol. 3 (London, 1801), 391.

92   "Peter Skunk" Thomas Paine, *A Letter to George Washington, on the Subject of the Late Treaty Concluded Between Great-Britain and the United States of America, Including Other Matters* (London, 1797), 27.

92   "Paine observed…" *Cobbett's Weekly Political Register* 27, no. 6 (11 February 1815) in *Cobbett's Political Register*, vol. 27, *From January to June, 1815* (London, 1815), 170.

93   "Paine lies…" William Cobbett to Lord Viscount Folkestone, 11 July 1819, in *Cobbett's Weekly Political Register* 35, no. 5 (18 September

1819) in *Cobbett's Political Register*, vol. 35, *Including the Time between August 14, 1819, and January 27, 1820* (London, 1820), 131–132.

93   "There, gentlemen…" *Times* (London), November 27, 1819.

93   "In digging up your bones…" Lord Byron, *Miscellanies*, vol. 3 (London: John Murray, 1837), 235.

BURR AND HAMILTON

95   "His private character…" Alexander Hamilton to Oliver Wolcott, 16 December 1800, in *The Papers of Alexander Hamilton*, vol. 25, *July 1800–April 1802*, ed. Harold C. Syrett (New York: Columbia University Press, 1977), 257.

96   "I am a dead man" Aaron Burr to Charles Biddle, 18 July 1804, in *Political Correspondence and Public Papers of Aaron Burr*, vol. 2, ed. Mary-Jo Kline (Princeton, NJ: Princeton University Press, 1983), 887.

97   "He is for or against…" Alexander Hamilton to unknown correspondent, 21 September 1792, in *The Papers of Alexander Hamilton*, vol. 12, *July 1792–October 1792*, ed. Harold C. Syrett (New York: Columbia University Press, 1967), 408.

97   "embryo-Caesar" Alexander Hamilton to unknown correspondent, 26 September 1792, in Syrett, *Papers of Hamilton*, 12:480.

98   "If you…really believe…" Aaron Burr to James Monroe, 13 August 1797, in *Political Correspondence and Public Papers of Aaron Burr*, vol. 1, ed. Mary-Jo Kline (Princeton, NJ: Princeton University Press, 1983), 312.

99   "There is no doubt…" and "As to Burr…" Hamilton to Wolcott in Syrett, *Papers of Hamilton*, 25:257.

100   "Nothing has given me so much chagrin…" and "He is certainly…" Alexander Hamilton to James McHenry, 4 January 1801, in Syrett, *Papers of Hamilton*, 25:292.

101   "The ill opinion…" Speech at a Meeting of Federalists in Albany, [10 February 1804], in *The Papers of Alexander Hamilton*, vol. 26, *May 1, 1802–October 23, 1804, Additional Documents 1774–1799, Addenda and Errata*, ed. Harold C. Syrett (New York: Columbia University Press, 1979), 189.

102   "a dangerous man…" and "I could detail to you…" "To Philip Schuyler, Esq.," *Albany (NY) Register*, 24 April 1804.

102   "the phrase…" Alexander Hamilton to Aaron Burr, 20 June 1804, in *Interview in Weehawken: The Burr-Hamilton Duel As Told in the Original Documents*, ed. Harold G. Syrett and Jean G. Cooke (Middletown, CT: Wesleyan University Press, 1960), 52.

102   "It is too well known…" Burr to Biddle in Kline, *Political Correspondence and Public Papers of Burr*, 2:887.

103   "no ill-will…" Alexander Hamilton's Remarks on His Impending Duel with Aaron Burr, [27 June–4 July 1804], in Syrett and Cooke, *Interview in Weehawken*, 99.

103   "my animadversions…" Ibid., 100.

104   "This world surely…" [Laurence Sterne], *The Life and Opinions of Tristram Shandy, Gentleman*, vol. 1 (London, 1794), 172.

104   "I should have known…" James Parton, *The Life and Times of Aaron Burr, Lieutenant-Colonel in the Army of the Revolution, United*

States Senator, Vice-President of the United States, etc., enlarged ed., vol. 2 (Boston: Houghton Mifflin, 1881), 322.

BURR AND JEFFERSON

105   "No man's history…" Thomas Jefferson to Robert R. Livingston, 25 March 1807, in *The Writings of Thomas Jefferson*, vol. 11, ed. Andrew A. Lipscomb (Washington, DC: Thomas Jefferson Memorial Association, 1903), 172.

105   "In New York…" Aaron Burr to Joseph Alston, 22 March 1805, in *Memoirs of Aaron Burr, with Miscellaneous Selections from His Correspondence*, vol. 2, ed. Matthew L. Davis (New York: Harper & Brothers, 1837), 365.

105   "beyond question" 16 Annals of Congress 40 (1807).

106   "It is highly improbable…" and "counteracting the Wishes…" Aaron Burr to Samuel Smith, 16 December 1800, in *Political Correspondence and Public Papers of Aaron Burr*, vol. 1, ed. Mary-Jo Kline (Princeton, NJ: Princeton University Press, 1983), 471.

107   "The question was…" Aaron Burr to Samuel Smith, 29 December 1800, in Kline, *Political Correspondence and Public Papers of Burr*, 1:479.

107   "holds to no pernicious…" Theodore Sedgwick to Alexander Hamilton, 10 January 1801, in *The Papers of Alexander Hamilton*, vol. 25, *July 1800–April 1802*, ed. Harold C. Syrett (New York: Columbia University Press, 1977), 311.

108   "reverse what has been understood…" Thomas Jefferson to Hugh

Henry Brackenridge, 18 December 1800, in *The Papers of Thomas Jefferson Digital Edition*, ed. Barbara B. Oberg and J. Jefferson Looney (Charlottesville: University of Virginia Press, Rotunda, 2008–2015), http://rotunda.upress.virginia.edu/founders/TSJN -01–32–02–0218.

108   "I never indeed…" Thomas Jefferson to William B. Giles, 20 April 1807, in Lipscomb, *Writings of Jefferson*, 11:191.

109   "the severance of the union…" 16 Annals of Cong. 41 (1807).

109   "Burr's enterprise…" Thomas Jefferson to Charles Clay, 11 January 1807, in Lipscomb, *Writings of Jefferson*, 11:133.

109   "No man's history…" Jefferson to Livingston in Lipscomb, *Writings of Jefferson*, 11:172.

111   "You see?…" James Parton, *The Life and Times of Aaron Burr, Lieutenant-Colonel in the Army of the Revolution,…* (New York: Mason Brothers, 1858), 670.

JEFFERSON AND MARSHALL

113   "The law is nothing more…" Thomas Jefferson to John Tyler, 26 May 1810, in *The Papers of Thomas Jefferson Digital Edition*, ed. Barbara B. Oberg and J. Jefferson Looney (Charlottesville: University of Virginia Press, Rotunda, 2008), http://rotunda.upress.virginia .edu/founders/TSJN-03–02–02–0365.

113   "He is among the most ambitious…" John Marshall to Joseph Story, 13 July 1821, in *The Papers of John Marshall*, vol. 9, *Correspondence, Papers, and Selected Judicial Opinions, January 1820–December 1823*, ed. Charles F. Hobson (Chapel Hill, NC: University of

North Carolina Press in association with the Institute of Early American History and Culture, 1998), 179.

113 "By all rights..." Joseph J. Ellis, *American Sphinx: The Character of Thomas Jefferson* (New York: Alfred A. Knopf, 1997), 175.

115 "I think nothing better..." Thomas Jefferson to James Madison, 29 June 1792, in Oberg and Looney, *Papers of Jefferson Digital Edition*, http://rotunda.upress.virginia.edu/founders/TSJN-01–24 –02–0134.

115 "lax lounging manners..." Thomas Jefferson to James Madison, 26 November 1795, in Oberg and Looney, *Papers of Jefferson Digital Edition*, http://rotunda.upress.virginia.edu/founders/TSJN-01–28 –02–0417.

116 "totally...unfit him..." and "the morals of the author..." John Marshall to Alexander Hamilton, 1 January 1801, in *The Papers of John Marshall*, vol. 6, *Correspondence, Papers, and Selected Judicial Opinions, November 1800–March 1807*, ed. Charles F. Hobson (Chapel Hill, NC: University of North Carolina Press in association with the Institute of Early American History and Culture, 1990), 46.

117 "The democrats are divided..." John Marshall to Charles Cotesworth Pinckney, 4 March 1801, in Hobson, *Papers of John Marshall*, 6:89.

117 "unite with one heart..." Thomas Jefferson, First Inaugural Address, 4 March 1801, in Oberg and Looney, *Papers of Jefferson Digital Edition*, http://rotunda.upress.virginia.edu/founders/TSJN-01–33–02 –0116–0004.

117 "well judged..." Marshall to Pinckney in Hobson, *Papers of John Marshall*, 6:89.

118   "An act of the legislature..." and "It is emphatically..." *Marbury v. Madison*, 5 U.S. 137, 178 (1803), in Hobson, *Papers of John Marshall*, 6:182, 183.

118   "beyond comparison..." "Number 78: A View of the Constitution of the Judicial Department, in Relation to the Tenure of Good Behaviour," *The Federalist: A Collection of Essays, Written in Favour of the New Constitution, as Agreed upon by the Federal Convention, September 17, 1787*, vol. 2 (New York, 1788), 292.

120   "overt act" *United States v. Burr*, 25 Fed. Cas. 55, 159 (31 August 1807), in *The Papers of John Marshall*, vol. 7, *Correspondence, Papers, and Selected Judicial Opinions, April 1807–December 1813*, ed. Charles F. Hobson (Chapel Hill, NC: University of North Carolina Press in association with the Institute of Early American History and Culture, 1993), 74.

120   "the hand of malignity..." *Burr*, 25 Fed. Cas. 2, 12, in Hobson, *Papers of John Marshall*, 7:13.

121   "We had supposed..." Thomas Jefferson to William Thomson, 26 September 1807, in *The Writings of Thomas Jefferson*, vol. 9, *1807–1815*, ed. Paul Leicester Ford (New York: G.P. Putnam's Sons, 1898), 143.

121   "we have long enough suffered..." Jefferson to Tyler in Oberg and Looney, *Papers of Jefferson Digital Edition*.

121   "twistifications..." Thomas Jefferson to James Madison, 25 May 1810, in Oberg and Looney, *Papers of Jefferson Digital Edition*, http://rotunda.upress.virginia.edu/founders/TSJN-03–02–02–0362.

121   "the subtle corps..." Thomas Jefferson to Thomas Ritchie, 25

December 1820, in *The Writings of Thomas Jefferson*, vol. 15, ed. Andrew A. Lipscomb (Washington, DC: Thomas Jefferson Memorial Association, 1903), 297.

122   "When conversing with Marshall…" Hayes, diary entry, 20 September 1843, in Charles Richard Williams, The *Life of Rutherford Birchard Hayes: Nineteenth President of the United States, vol. 1 (Boston: Houghton Mifflin, 1914)*, 33. Williams includes entries from Hayes's diary, including Hayes's notes on lectures Story gave at Harvard Law School.

122   "For Mr. Jefferson's opinion…" Marshall to Story in Hobson, *Papers of Marshall*, 9:179.

JEFFERSON AND RANDOLPH

123   "The old Republican Party…" John Randolph to George Hay, 3 January 1806, John Randolph of Roanoke Papers, 1781–1860, Special Collections, University of Virginia Library, Charlottesville.

123   "The example of John Randolph…" Thomas Jefferson to William Duane, 30 April 1811, in *The Papers of Thomas Jefferson Digital Edition*, ed. Barbara B. Oberg and J. Jefferson Looney (Charlottesville: University of Virginia Press, Rotunda, 2008), http://rotunda.upress .virginia.edu/founders/TSJN-03–03–02–0464.

124   "Mr. Randolph goes to the House…" William Plumer to William Plumer Jr., 22 February 1803, in William Plumer Jr., *Life of William Plumer*, ed. A. P. Peabody (Boston: Phillips, Sampson, 1857), 256.

124   "popular eloquence…" and "humiliations he subjected them to" Thomas Jefferson to James Monroe, 4 May 1806, in *The Papers of James Monroe: Selected Correspondence and Papers*, vol. 5, January 1803–April 1811, ed. Daniel Preston (Santa Barbara, CA: Greenwood, 2014), 472.

124   "brilliant" Powhatan Bouldin, *Home Reminiscences of John Randolph of Roanoke* (Danville, VA, 1876), 303n.

125   "What is the spirit…" and "A monster generated by fraud…" 14 Annals of Cong. 1032 (1805).

125   "But when I see…" Ibid.

126   "did not know what course…" *William Plumer's Memorandum of Proceedings in the United States Senate, 1803–1807*, ed. Everett Somerville Brown (New York: MacMillan, 1923), 370.

126   "without order, connection, or argument…" *Memoirs of John Quincy Adams, Comprising Portions of His Diary from 1795 to 1848*, vol. 1, ed. Charles Francis Adams (Philadelphia: J. B. Lippincott, 1874), 359.

127   "the mask which ambition…" John Randolph to James Mercer Garnett, 4 September 1806, in John Randolph of Roanoke Papers, 1781–1860, Special Collections, University of Virginia Library, Charlottesville.

127   "past redemption" and "New men…" Randolph to Hay, John Randolph of Roanoke Papers.

127   "I came here prepared to cooperate…" 15 Annals of Congress 984 (1806).

127   "The defection of so prominent…" Thomas Jefferson to Wilson C.

Nicholas, 13 April 1806, in *The Writings of Thomas Jefferson*, vol. 11, ed. Andrew A. Lipscomb (Washington, DC: Thomas Jefferson Memorial Association, 1903), 99–100.

127   "a state of as perfect…" Thomas Jefferson to James Monroe in Preston, *Papers of James Monroe*, 5:472.

128   "bold and unauthorized assertions" Thomas Jefferson to William A. Burwell, 17 September 1806, in *The Writings of Thomas Jefferson*, vol. 8, *1801–1806*, ed. Paul Leicester Ford (New York: G. P. Putnam's Sons, 1897), 469.

128   "How different is the stake…" Thomas Jefferson to Thomas Mann Randolph, 23 June 1806, Edgehill-Randolph Papers, 1749 (1790–1850) 1886, acc. #1397, Special Collections, University of Virginia Library, Charlottesville.

129   "outcast" and "a caution…" Jefferson to Duane in Oberg and Looney, *Papers of Jefferson Digital Edition*.

129   "cancer" 2 Register of Debates 117 (1826).

129   "When men are furiously…" 2 Reg. Deb. 119 (1826).

130   "reprieve only" and "have the wolf…" Thomas Jefferson to John Holms, 22 April 1820, in *The Writings of Thomas Jefferson*, vol. 10, *1816–1826*, ed. Paul Leicester Ford (New York: G. P. Putnam's Sons, 1899), 157–158.

130   "companions in sentiments…" Thomas Jefferson to Edward Livingston, 4 April 1824, in Ford, *Writings of Jefferson*, 10:300.

JEFFERSON AND WHEATLEY

131   "Religion…has produced…" *Notes on the State of Virginia by Thomas*

Jefferson with Related Documents, ed. David Waldstreicher (Boston: Bedford/St. Martin's, 2002), 178.

132   "most respectable…" Phillis Wheatley, *Poems on Various Subjects, Religious and Moral* (London, 1773), 8.

132   "We whose names…" Ibid.

133   "Upon your recommendation…" Benjamin Franklin to Jonathan Williams Sr., 7 July 1773, in *The Papers of Benjamin Franklin*, vol. 20, *January 1 through December 31, 1773*, ed. William B. Willcox (New Haven: Yale University Press, 1976), 291–292.

134   "Proceed, great chief…" Poem by Phillis Wheatley (enclosure), Phillis Wheatley to George Washington, 26 October 1775, in *The Papers of George Washington Digital Edition*, ed. Theodore J. Crackel (Charlottesville: University of Virginia Press, Rotunda, 2008), http://rotunda.upress.virginia.edu/founders/GEWN-03–02–02 –0222–0002.

134   "the elegant lines…" and "while I only meant to give…" George Washington to Phillis Wheatley, 28 February 1776, in Crackel, *Papers of Washington Digital Edition*, http://rotunda.upress.virginia .edu/founders/GEWN-03–03–02–0281.

135   "Among the blacks…" *Notes on the State of Virginia by Jefferson*, 178.

136   "they were of the race…" Ibid., 179.

136   "The whole commerce…" and "And can the liberties…" Ibid., 195.

136   "the slave rising from the dust…" Ibid., 196.

136   "Why not retain…" Ibid., 175–176.

137   "superior intellectual camouflage" David Grimsted, "Anglo-American Racism and Phillis Wheatley's 'Sable Veil,' Length'ned Chain,' and

'Knitted Heart,'" in *Women in the Age of the American Revolution*, ed. Ronald Hoffman and Peter J. Albert (Charlottesville: University Press of Virginia, 1989), 425.

137 "while they wish to vindicate…" John Burk, *The History of Virginia, from Its First Settlement to the Present Day*, vol. 1 (Petersburg, VA, 1804), 212n.

137 "an opportunity…" and "Phillis appears…" G[ilbert] Imlay, *A Topographical Description of the Western Territory of North America…* (London, 1792), 198.

137 "For let no one of us suppose…" [David Walker], *Walker's Appeal, in Four Articles, Together with a Preamble to the Colored Citizens of the World, but in Particular and Very Expressly to Those of the United States of America* (Boston, 1829), 16.

138 "became the strongest motivation…" Henry Louis Gates Jr., *The Trials of Phillis Wheatley: America's First Black Poet and Her Encounters with the Founding Fathers* (New York: Basic Books, 2010), 51.

138 "If Phillis Wheatley was the mother…" Ibid., 50.

138 "pleasant imitations…" LeRoi Jones [Amiri Baraka], *Home: Social Essays* (New York: William Morrow, 1966), 106.

138 "In every human breast…" and "How well the cry…" Phillis Wheatley, *Complete Writings*, ed. Vincent Carretta (New York: Penguin, 2001), 153.

139 "The African-American poet who seems…" David Waldstreicher, "Phillis Wheatley: The Poet Who Challenged the American Revolutionaries," in *Revolutionary Founders: Rebels, Radicals, and*

Reformers in the Making of the Nation, ed. Alfred F. Young, Gary B. Nash, and Ray Raphael (New York: Vintage Books, 2012), 112.

ADAMS AND WARREN

141   "His prejudices and his passions…" Mercy Warren, *History of the Rise, Progress and Termination of the American Revolution Interspersed with Biographical, Political and Moral Observations*, vol. 3 (Boston, 1805), 392.

141   "If Mrs. Warren is determined…" John Adams to Mercy Warren, 15 August 1807, in "Correspondence between John Adams and Mercy Warren Relating to Her 'History of the American Revolution,' July–August, 1807," part 3 in *Collections of the Massachusetts Historical Society*, fifth series, vol. 4 (Boston, 1878), 464.

142   "pride of talents…" and "a partiality for monarchy" Warren, *History of the American Revolution*, 3:393, 394.

143   "celebrated by a certain poetical pen…" John Adams to James Warren, 22 December 1773, in *Papers of John Adams*, vol. 2, *December 1773–April 1775*, ed. Robert J. Taylor (Cambridge, MA: Belknap Press of Harvard University Press, 1977), 3.

143   "one of the most incontestable…" John Adams to James Warren, 9 April 1774, in Taylor, *Papers of John Adams*, 2:82.

143   "Of all the geniuses…" John Adams to Mercy Otis Warren, 15 March 1775 in Taylor, *Papers of John Adams*, 2:408.

143   "It was best for a general rule…" John Adams to James Warren, 26 September 1775, in *Papers of John Adams*, vol. 3, *May 1775–January*

1776, ed. Robert J. Taylor (Cambridge, MA: Belknap Press of Harvard University Press, 1979), 168.

143 "taxation without representation…" John Adams to William Tudor, 5 April 1818, in *The Works of John Adams, Second President of the United States: With a Life of the Author, Notes and Illustrations*, vol. 10, ed. Charles Francis Adams (Boston: Little, Brown, 1856), 303.

144 "conscious of its inferiority…" John Adams to Mercy Otis Warren, 3 January 1775, in Taylor, *Papers of John Adams*, 2:210.

144 "give up so important…" Abigail Adams to Mercy Otis Warren, 14 August 1777, in *The Adams Papers Digital Edition*, ed. C. James Taylor (Charlottesville: University of Virginia Press, Rotunda), 2008–2015, http://rotunda.upress.virginia.edu/founders/ADMS -04–02–02–0252.

144 "many-headed monster…" [Mercy Warren], *Observations on the New Constitution, and on the Federal and State Conventions* (Boston: 1788), 7.

145 "General Warren did differ…" and "belie the whole course…" John Adams to Mercy Warren, 29 May 1789, in *Warren-Adams Letters: Being Chiefly a Correspondence among John Adams, Samuel Adams, and James Warren*, vol. 2, *1778–1814* (Boston: Massachusetts Historical Society, 1925; repr., New York: AMS Press, 1972), 313, 314.

145 "in a country…" Abigail Adams to Mercy Warren, 4 March 1797, in *Warren-Adams Letters*, 2:332.

146 "Mr. Adams was undoubtedly…" Warren, *History of the American Revolution*, 3:392.

146 "unfortunately for himself..." and "he was implicated..." Ibid.

147 "beclouded" and "It may...be charitably presumed..." Ibid., 394.

147 "no doubt the work..." Thomas Jefferson to Mercy Warren, 8 February 1805, *Warren-Adams Letters*, 2:345.

147 "I am not conscious..." John Adams to Mercy Adams, 11 July 1807, in "Correspondence between Adams and Warren," 4:322.

148 "absolute monarchy," "absolute democracy," "always advocated...," and "would not recommend..." Ibid., 325.

148 "I have done more labor..." John Adams to Mercy Warren, 19 August 1807, in "Correspondence between Adams and Warren," 4:470.

148 "Most of these..." John Adams to Mercy Warren, 15 August 1807, in "Correspondence between Adams and Warren," 4:464.

148 "What have I done..." John Adams to Mercy Warren, 30 July 1807, in "Correspondence between Adams and Warren," 4:394.

148 "Angry as you have appeared..." Mercy Warren to John Adams, 15 August 1807, in "Correspondence between Adams and Warren," 4:448.

149 "I have uniformly endeavored..." Mercy Adams to John Adams, 16 July 1807, in "Correspondence between Adams and Warren," 4:329.

149 "Had not Mr. Adams..." Mercy Warren to John Adams, 28 July 1807, in "Correspondence between Adams and Warren," 4:360.

149 "The history has gone forth..." Mercy Warren to John Adams, 27 August 1807, in "Correspondence between Adams and Warren," 4:489.

150 "that of your ancient friend's..." Abigail Adams to Mercy Warren,

30 December 1812, in "Correspondence between Adams and Warren," 4:502.

150 "History is not the province…" John Adams to Elbridge Gerry, 17 April 1813, in *Warren-Adams Letters*, 2:380.

EPILOGUE

152 "the closest thing…" Jon Meacham, *Thomas Jefferson: The Art of Power* (New York: Random House, 2012), 500.

152 "the birthday of…" Thomas Paine, *Common Sense; Addressed to the Inhabitants of America, on the Following Interesting Subjects…* (Philadelphia, 1776), 47.

152 "Despite all his shortcomings…" Meacham, *Thomas Jefferson*, 500.

FURTHER READING

DEANE AND LEE

Lefer, David. *The Founding Conservatives: How a Group of Unsung Heroes Saved the American Revolution*. New York: Sentinel, 2013.

Nagel, Paul C. *The Lees of Virginia: Seven Generations of an American Family*. New York: Oxford University Press, 1990.

Paul, Joel Richard. *Unlikely Allies: How a Merchant, a Playwright, and a Spy Saved the American Revolution*. New York: Riverhead Books, 2009.

Potts, Louis W. *Arthur Lee: A Virtuous Revolutionary*. Baton Rouge: Louisiana State University Press, 1981.

Rakove, Jack N. *The Beginnings of National Politics: An Interpretive History of the Continental Congress*. New York: Alfred A. Knopf, 1979.

WASHINGTON AND WASHINGTON

Brookhiser, Richard. *Founding Father: Rediscovering George Washington*. New York: Free Press, 1996.

Burns, James MacGregor, and Susan Dunn. *George Washington*. New York: Times Books, 2004.

Chernow, Ron. *Washington: A Life*. New York: Penguin, 2010.

Countryman, Edward. *Enjoy the Same Liberty: Black Americans and the Revolutionary Era*. Lanham, MD: Rowman & Littlefield, 2012.

Egerton, Douglas R. *Death or Liberty: African Americans and Revolutionary America*. New York: Oxford University Press, 2009.

Gilbert, Alan. *Black Patriots and Loyalists: Fighting for Emancipation in the War for Independence*. Chicago: University of Chicago Press, 2012.

Holton, Woody. *Forced Founders: Indians, Debtors, Slaves, and the Making of the American Revolution in Virginia*. Chapel Hill: University of North Carolina Press, 1999.

Nash, Gary B. *The Forgotten Fifth: African Americans and the Age of Revolution*. Cambridge, MA: Harvard University Press, 2006.

Pybus, Cassandra. *Epic Journeys of Freedom: Runaway Slaves of the American Revolution and Their Global Quest for Liberty*. Boston: Beacon Press, 2006.

Schama, Simon. *Rough Crossings: Britain, the Slaves, and the American Revolution*. New York: Ecco, 2006.

LINCOLN AND SHAYS

Gross, Robert A., ed. *In Debt to Shays: The Bicentennial of an Agrarian Rebellion*. Charlottesville: University Press of Virginia, 1993.

Holton, Woody. *Unruly Americans and the Origins of the Constitution*. New York: Hill and Wang, 2007.

Mattern, David B. *Benjamin Lincoln and the American Revolution*. Columbia: University of South Carolina Press, 1995.

Nobles, Gregory. "'Satan, Smith, Shattuck, and Shays': The People's Leaders in the Massachusetts Regulation of 1786." In *Revolutionary*

Founders: Rebels, Radicals, and Reformers in the Making of the Nation, ed. Alfred F. Young, Gary B. Nash, and Ray Raphael, 215–231. New York: Alfred A. Knopf, 2011.

Richards, Leonard L. *Shays's Rebellion: The American Revolution's Final Battle.* Philadelphia: University of Pennsylvania Press, 2002.

Szatmary, David P. *Shays's Rebellion: The Making of an Agrarian Insurrection.* Amherst: University of Massachusetts Press, 1980.

HENRY AND MADISON

Broadwater, Jeff. *James Madison: A Son of Virginia and a Founder of the Nation.* Chapel Hill: University of North Carolina Press, 2012.

Brookhiser, Richard. *James Madison.* New York: Basic Books, 2011.

Ellis, Joseph J. *American Creation: Triumphs and Tragedies at the Founding of the Republic.* New York: Alfred A. Knopf, 2007.

Henry, William Wirt. *Patrick Henry: Life, Correspondence and Speeches.* Vol. 2. New York: Burt Franklin, 1969. First published 1891.

Kidd, Thomas S. *Patrick Henry: First Among Patriots.* New York: Basic Books, 2011.

Maier, Pauline. *Ratification: The People Debate the Constitution, 1787–1788.* New York: Simon & Schuster, 2010.

Meacham, Jon. *Thomas Jefferson: The Art of Power.* New York: Random House, 2012.

Signer, Michael. *Becoming Madison: The Extraordinary Origins of the Least Likely Founding Father.* New York: Public Affairs, 2015.

Unger, Harlow Giles. *Lion of Liberty: Patrick Henry and the Call to a New Nation.* Boston: Da Capo Press, 2010.

Wirt, William. *Sketches of the Life and Character of Patrick Henry*. Philadelphia: James Webster, 1817.

HAMILTON AND JEFFERSON

Chernow, Ron. *Alexander Hamilton*. New York: Penguin, 2004.

Ellis, Joseph J. *American Sphinx: The Character of Thomas Jefferson*. New York: Alfred A. Knopf, 1997.

Ferling, John. *Jefferson and Hamilton: The Rivalry That Forged a Nation*. New York: Bloomsbury Press, 2013.

Kennedy, Roger G. *Burr, Hamilton, and Jefferson: A Study in Character*. New York: Oxford University Press, 2000.

Meacham, Jon. *Thomas Jefferson: The Art of Power*. New York: Random House, 2012.

Staloff, Darren. *Hamilton, Adams, Jefferson: The Politics of Enlightenment and the American Founding*. New York: Hill and Wang, 2005.

ADAMS AND JEFFERSON

Dunn, Susan. *Jefferson's Second Revolution: The Election Crisis of 1800 and the Triumph of Republicanism*. Boston: Houghton Mifflin, 2004.

Ellis, Joseph J. *Founding Brothers: The Revolutionary Generation*. New York: Alfred A. Knopf, 2000.

Ferling, John. *Adams vs. Jefferson: The Tumultuous Election of 1800*. New York: Oxford University Press, 2004.

Horn, James, Jan Ellen Lewis, and Peter S. Onuf, eds. *The Revolution of 1800: Democracy, Race, and the New Republic*. Charlottesville: University of Virginia Press, 2002.

Larson, Edward J. *A Magnificent Catastrophe: The Tumultuous Election of 1800, America's First Presidential Campaign*. New York: Free Press, 2007.

McCullough, David. *John Adams*. New York: Simon & Schuster, 2001.

Meacham, Jon. *Thomas Jefferson: The Art of Power*. New York: Random House, 2012.

ADAMS AND HAMILTON

Beschloss, Michael. *Presidential Courage: Brave Leaders and How They Changed America, 1789–1989*. New York: Simon & Schuster, 2007.

Chernow, Ron. *Alexander Hamilton*. New York: Penguin, 2004.

Elkins, Stanley, and Eric McKitrick. *The Age of Federalism: The Early American Republic, 1788–1800*. New York: Oxford University Press, 1993.

Ellis, Joseph J. *Passionate Sage: The Character and Legacy of John Adams*. New York: W.W. Norton, 1993. Reissued with new preface 2001.

Freeman, Joanne B. *Affairs of Honor: National Politics in the New Republic*. New Haven, CT: Yale University Press, 2001.

Grant, James. *John Adams: Party of One*. New York: Farrar, Straus and Giroux, 2005.

McCullough, David. *John Adams*. New York: Simon & Schuster, 2001.

PAINE AND WASHINGTON

Brookhiser, Richard. *Founding Father: Rediscovering George Washington*. New York: Free Press, 1996.

Chernow, Ron. *Washington: A Life*. New York: Penguin, 2010.

Ellis, Joseph J. *His Excellency: George Washington*. New York: Alfred A. Knopf, 2004.

Foner, Eric. *Tom Paine and Revolutionary America*. New York: Oxford University Press, 1976.

Fruchtman, Jack, Jr. *The Political Philosophy of Thomas Paine*. Baltimore, MD: Johns Hopkins University Press, 2009.

———. *Thomas Paine: Apostle of Freedom*. New York: Four Walls Eight Windows, 1994.

Kahler, Gerald E. *The Long Farewell: Americans Mourn the Death of George Washington*. Charlottesville: University of Virginia Press, 2008.

Kaye, Harvey J. *Thomas Paine and the Promise of America*. New York: Hill and Wang, 2005.

Keane, John. *Tom Paine: A Political Life*. New York: Grove Press, 2007. First published 1995 by Bloomsbury, London.

Lengel, Edward G. *Inventing George Washington: America's Founder, in Myth and Memory*. New York: Harper Collins, 2011.

Nelson, Craig. *Thomas Paine: Enlightenment, Revolution, and the Birth of Modern Nations*. New York: Viking, 2006.

Rosenfeld, Sophia. *Common Sense: A Political History*. Cambridge, MA: Harvard University Press, 2011.

GRISWOLD AND LYON

Austin, Aleine. *Matthew Lyon: "New Man" of the Democratic Revolution, 1749–1822*. University Park: Pennsylvania State University Press, 1981.

Buel, Richard, Jr. *Securing the Revolution: Ideology in American Politics, 1789–1815*. Ithaca, NY: Cornell University Press, 1972.

Elkins, Stanley, and Eric McKitrick. *The Age of Federalism: The Early American Republic, 1788–1800*. New York: Oxford University Press, 1993.

Freeman, Joanne B. *Affairs of Honor: National Politics in the New Republic.* New Haven, CT: Yale University Press, 2001.

Pasley, Jeffrey L. *"The Tyranny of Printers": Newspaper Politics in the Early American Republic.* Charlottesville: University Press of Virginia, 2001.

Wood, Gordon S. *Empire of Liberty: A History of the Early Republic, 1789–1815.* New York: Oxford University Press, 2009.

COBBETT AND PAINE

Collins, Paul. *The Trouble with Tom: The Strange Afterlife and Times of Thomas Paine.* New York: Bloomsbury, 2005.

Foner, Eric. *Tom Paine and Revolutionary America.* New York: Oxford University Press, 1976.

Ford, Worthington Chauncey, ed. *Statesman and Friend: Correspondence of John Adams with Benjamin Waterhouse, 1784–1822.* Boston: Little, Brown, 1927.

Kaye, Harvey J. *Thomas Paine and the Promise of America.* New York: Hill and Wang, 2005.

Keane, John. *Tom Paine: A Political Life.* New York: Grove Press, 2007. First published 1995 by Bloomsbury, London.

Nelson, Craig. *Thomas Paine: Enlightenment, Revolution, and the Birth of Modern Nations.* New York: Viking, 2006.

Pasley, Jeffrey L. *"The Tyranny of Printers": Newspaper Politics in the Early American Republic.* Charlottesville: University Press of Virginia, 2001.

Wilson, David A. *Paine and Cobbett: The Transatlantic Connection.* Montreal and Kingston, Canada: McGill-Queen's University Press, 1988.

BURR AND HAMILTON

Brookhiser, Richard. *Alexander Hamilton, American*. New York: Free Press, 1999.

Chernow, Ron. *Alexander Hamilton*. New York: Penguin, 2004.

Ellis, Joseph J. *Founding Brothers: The Revolutionary Generation*. New York: Alfred A. Knopf, 2000.

Fleming, Thomas. *Duel: Alexander Hamilton, Aaron Burr and the Future of America*. New York: Basic Books, 1999.

Freeman, Joanne B. *Affairs of Honor: National Politics in the New Republic*. New Haven, CT: Yale University Press, 2001.

Isenberg, Nancy. *Fallen Founder: The Life of Aaron Burr*. New York: Viking, 2007.

Rogow, Arnold A. *A Fatal Friendship: Alexander Hamilton and Aaron Burr*. New York: Hill and Wang, 1998.

Wood, Gordon S. *Revolutionary Characters: What Made the Founders Different*. New York: Penguin, 2006.

BURR AND JEFFERSON

Dunn, Susan. *Jefferson's Second Revolution: The Election Crisis of 1800 and the Triumph of Republicanism*. Boston: Houghton Mifflin, 2004.

Ferling, John. *Adams vs. Jefferson: The Tumultuous Election of 1800*. New York: Oxford University Press, 2004.

Isenberg, Nancy. *Fallen Founder: The Life of Aaron Burr*. New York: Viking, 2007.

Kennedy, Roger G. *Burr, Hamilton, and Jefferson: A Study in Character*. New York: Oxford University Press, 2000.

Meacham, Jon. *Thomas Jefferson: The Art of Power*. New York: Random House, 2012.

Melton, Buckner F., Jr. *Aaron Burr: Conspiracy to Treason*. New York: John Wiley & Sons, 2002.

Sharp, James Roger. *The Deadlocked Election of 1800: Jefferson, Burr, and the Union in the Balance*. Lawrence: University Press of Kansas, 2010.

Stewart, David O. *American Emperor: Aaron Burr's Challenge to Jefferson's America*. New York: Simon & Schuster, 2011.

JEFFERSON AND MARSHALL

Ellis, Joseph J. *American Sphinx: The Character of Thomas Jefferson*. New York: Alfred A. Knopf, 1997.

Meacham, Jon. *Thomas Jefferson: The Art of Power*. New York: Random House, 2012.

Newmyer, R. Kent. *John Marshall and the Heroic Age of the Supreme Court*. Baton Rouge: Louisiana State University Press, 2001.

Paul, Joel Richard. *Without Precedent*. New York: Riverhead, forthcoming.

Robarge, David. *A Chief Justice's Progress: John Marshall from Revolutionary Virginia to the Supreme Court*. Westport, CT: Greenwood Press, 2000.

Smith, Jean Edward. *John Marshall: Definer of a Nation*. New York: Henry Holt, 1996.

JEFFERSON AND RANDOLPH

Appleby, Joyce. *Thomas Jefferson*. New York: Times Books, 2003.

Bouldin, Powhatan. *Home Reminiscences of John Randolph of Roanoke*. Danville and Richmond, VA, 1878.

Dawidoff, Robert. *The Education of John Randolph*. New York: W.W. Norton, 1979.

Howe, Daniel Walker. *What Hath God Wrought: The Transformation of America, 1815–1848*. New York: Oxford University Press, 2007.

Johnson, David. *John Randolph of Roanoke*. Baton Rouge: Louisiana State University Press, 2012.

Meacham, Jon. *Thomas Jefferson: The Art of Power*. New York: Random House, 2012.

JEFFERSON AND WHEATLEY

Carretta, Vincent. *Phillis Wheatley: Biography of a Genius in Bondage*. Athens: University of Georgia Press, 2011.

Gates, Henry Louis, Jr. *The Trials of Phillis Wheatley: America's First Black Poet and Her Encounters with the Founding Fathers*. New York: Basic Civitas Books, 2003.

Grimsted, David. "Anglo-American Racism and Phillis Wheatley's 'Sable Veil,' Length'ned Chain,' and 'Knitted Heart.'" In *Women in the Age of the American Revolution*, ed. Ronald Hoffman and Peter J. Albert, 338–444. Charlottesville: University Press of Virginia, 1989.

Miller, John Chester. *The Wolf by the Ears: Thomas Jefferson and Slavery*. New York: Free Press, 1977.

Waldstreicher, David. "Phillis Wheatley: The Poet Who Challenged the American Revolutionaries." In *Revolutionary Founders: Rebels, Radicals, and Reformers in the Making of the Nation*, ed. by Alfred F. Young, Gary B. Nash, and Ray Raphael, 97–113. New York: Alfred A. Knopf, 2011.

Wheatley, Phillis. *Complete Writings*. Edited by Vincent Carretta. New York: Penguin, 2001.

ADAMS AND WARREN

Davies, Kate. *Catharine Macaulay and Mercy Otis Warren: The Revolutionary Atlantic and the Politics of Gender*. New York: Oxford University Press, 2005.

McCullough, David. *John Adams*. New York: Simon & Schuster, 2001.

Richards, Jeffrey H. *Mercy Otis Warren*. New York: Twayne, 1995.

Stuart, Nancy Rubin. *The Muse of the Revolution: The Secret Pen of Mercy Otis Warren and the Founding of a Nation*. Boston: Beacon Press, 2008.

Zagarri, Rosemarie. *A Woman's Dilemma: Mercy Otis Warren and the American Revolution*. Wheeling, IL: Harlan Davidson, 1995.

ACKNOWLEDGMENTS

I AM GRATEFUL FOR THE HELP OF STEPHEN ARON, STEPHANIE BOWEN, Joel Paul, Joseph Thomas, and Amy Watson. Thanks also to Grace Menary-Winefield for her supportive yet incisive editing.

The idea for this book grew out of *The Idea of America*, an online program developed by the Colonial Williamsburg Foundation. The program and an accompanying book, written by H. Michael Hartoonian, Richard D. Van Scotter, and William E. White, present American history as a great debate through which each generation has attempted to balance four "value tensions": private wealth and common wealth; freedom and equality; unity and diversity; law and ethics. I am indebted to Hartoonian, Van Scotter, and White for inspiring me to think about the extent to which our nation, from its origins to the present, has been shaped by our disagreements, even by our feuds.

PHOTO CREDITS

Portrait of James Monroe
John Vanderlyn
District of Columbia, 1816
Oil on canvas
Museum Purchase, 1946–80

Portrait of Patrick Henry
Thomas Sully
Philadelphia, Pennsylvania, 1815
Oil on canvas
Museum Purchase, 1958–3

Portrait of George Washington
Attributed to Gilbert Stuart
Philadelphia, Pennsylvania (probably), 1796–1803
Oil on canvas
Gift of Marilyn Brown and Douglas Morton in honor of
    Colin G. and Nancy N. Campbell, 2014–203.

INDEX

ABOUT THE AUTHOR

PAUL ARON IS DIRECTOR OF PUBLICATIONS AT THE COLONIAL Williamsburg Foundation. He is the author of *Unsolved Mysteries of American History*, *Unsolved Mysteries of History*, *Count the Ways*, *More Unsolved Mysteries of American History*, *Did Babe Ruth Call His Shot?*, *Mysteries in History*, *We Hold These Truths…*, and *Why the Turkey Didn't Fly*.

ABOUT COLONIAL WILLIAMSBURG

The Colonial Williamsburg Foundation is the not-for-profit center for history and citizenship, encouraging audiences at home and around the world to learn from the past.

Colonial Williamsburg is dedicated to the preservation, restoration, and presentation of eighteenth-century Williamsburg and the study, interpretation, and teaching of America's founding principles. The foundation operates the 301-acre restored eighteenth-century capital of Virginia.